Dane Mutter

nature
in
dayton

An Anthology

The views and opinions expressed in this work are those of the author and do not necessarily reflect the views and opinions of Braughler Books LLC.

info@braughlerbooks.com

Cover photo: iStock.com/StanRohrer

Printed in the United States of America
Published by Braughler Books LLC., Springboro, Ohio

First printing, 2020

ISBN: 978-1-970063-65-3

Library of Congress Control Number: 2020912373

Ordering information: Special discounts are available on quantity purchases by bookstores, corporations, associations, and others. For details, contact the publisher at:

sales@braughlerbooks.com

or at 937-58-BOOKS

For questions or comments about this book, please write to:

info@braughlerbooks.com

Braughler™
Books
braughlerbooks.com

Contents

Contents

Introduction

Dayton owes its beginning to natural phenomena—three rivers: the Mad, the Stillwater, and the Great Miami.

The exact date is April 1, 1796. Imagine yourself in a pirogue, a raft-like vessel being poled and paddled upstream in April. You're tired, chilled, and badly in need of a pit stop.

A score of people jumped from the pirogue. The party included Samuel Thompson, Benjamin Van Cleve, and little nine-year-old Mary Van Cleve. Four days later another group arrived that had been travelling on foot from Cincinnati, led by Colonel George Newcomb. A few days later a third party made its appearance. The site is now marked at Van Cleve Park. That was 224 years ago.

When Priscilla and I located at 807 Riverview Terrace overlooking the Great Miami River, we were within walking distance of central downtown. We often walked over to the Arcade for lunch or dinner. My curiosity as a naturalist posed questions. "Is there anything wild about downtown besides starlings, ailanthus trees and pigeons? Just what is natural about downtown Dayton?" The deeper I dug, the more surprising it became.

In September 1982, walking down the outside steps from Elder-Beerman to street level I heard a scuffling, scrambling noise from the eye-level trough that carried rainwater off the steps. I reached in and gently grasped a bewildered, frightened brown creeper, a little bird weighing about three tenths of an ounce. It seemed OK, so I let it go. It made a B-line to north Texas for winter. This was one of the early inspirations for my column.

The late columnist Jean Kappel encouraged the idea of a *Downtown Naturalist* column. Jim Van Dyne reviewed some of my writings and referred them to Jim Nichols, editor of the *Downtowner*. After 650 columns there was still plenty to write about.

In my last column, November 29, 1995, my editor, the late Jim Nichols, said "The *Downtown Naturalist* has been a unique reading experience for the downtown readers. Dane Mutter has worked hard to write it week after week. He may now, indeed, write a book. For his past efforts we thank him. For his dreams, we hope they all come true."

Here's the book. ▪

Talk with Dam Builder's Son Allows Time to Recall Dayton's Great Disaster of 1913

MARCH 30, 1988

The other evening I had the good fortune to chat with Ernest Morgan, Arthur Morgan's son. Arthur Morgan was the creative genius who designed the five flood control dams that have protected Dayton from flooding since they were completed in the late teens and early 1920s. Ernest is a healthy 83 years and is still active on the board of the Antioch Publishing Company.

We were discussing the 75th anniversary of the colossal 1913 flood that nearly washed Dayton off the map. "My father, Arthur Morgan, was an intensely creative man whose activities had a lasting impact in several areas of Miami Valley life. He came to Dayton to build the dams," Morgan said, "then he became President of the Board of the First Unitarian Church, and then President of Antioch College, and the rest is history."

Dayton Daily News, March 10, 1913—*From strangers who have come to offer aid there is astonished comment about the abounding good cheer that prevails. Thousands of families have seen fortunes slip away in a day. There is not a family in Dayton whose plans for the future have not been warped, some beyond repair. Yet smiling faces and courageous words prevail.*

Seventy-five years ago today these words exemplified the attitude and spirit of the people of Dayton as they began the

3

monstrous task of cleaning up after what is still the greatest disaster to strike our city.

The floodwaters peaked on March 26, after a deluge of rain totaling between nine and eleven inches fell between March 23 and March 27. The lethal combination of heavy rain and frozen ground resulted in 87 percent of the water running off, causing the flood.

Dayton Daily News, March 29, 1913—*Thousands of men, women and children who through curiosity risked their lives early Tuesday morning in watching the rising river at Monument Avenue and Main Street, fled in terror, south of Main Street when the water suddenly poured over the levee in the rear of the Legler property on Monument Avenue.*

Only a small quantity of water came over the levee, but the cry of terror that arose caused the crowds to become panic stricken. Fearing that wall of water, which would drown them if they were caught, was close behind them, they rushed pell-mell down the street.

A real danger met the fleeing thousand as they arrived at Third and Main Streets where water, rushing from a break in the levee at Webster Street, met them. Some were knee deep in water before they took refuge in office buildings along the street. As the flood reached the deep excavation at the corner of Fourth and Main Streets, it poured over the walls like a small Niagara. Within ten minutes after the first warning cry had started the crowd rushing down the street, there was five feet of water over all the streets in the center of the business district.

History, indeed, and it probably would have been repeated in 1937 and 1957, had not Dayton's first citizen, John H. Patterson, and the man he appointed as chairman of the Flood Prevention

Committee in 1913, Edward A. Deeds, tolerated an innovative and creative engineer, humanist and educator, named Morgan, to size up and solve the problem of flood control in the Miami Valley.

James Rozelle, now serving as chief engineer and general manager of the Miami Conservancy District, said "Dayton's system of the five flood control dams is unique, and attracts decision makers worldwide who wish to accomplish in their communities what Dayton did 75 years ago." ▪

Downtown Park Recalls
Historic April 1 Event

APRIL 2, 1986

Van Cleve Park lies at the head of St. Clair Street and extends to Jefferson Street one block west.

It is bordered on the north by the Great Miami River, and on the south, by Monument Avenue.

Here, on a warm sunny day last week, we heard the first house finch of spring singing its warbling song from a large ginkgo tree.

Another male finch was singing across Monument Avenue in a tree in front of the Engineer's Club. Crows and grackles perched in another tree, while robins probed the soft ground for fresh worms.

This green strip park, on the banks of the Great Miami, is a tree-covered emerald set in the fabric of the central business district. The first settlers climbed up the riverbank here after a tortuous ten-day trip up the Miami from Cincinnati.

Samuel Thompson was the leader of the party that landed here 190 year ago on April 1, 1796. Their mode of travel was a long, narrow pirogue, pointed on each end with boards on either side, which men walked while poling the boat upstream.

These exciting excerpts about Dayton's first settlers are from Professor William B. Werthner's paper, "The Backgrounds of Early Dayton History," which he presented to the Torch Club on the evening of November 13, 1928.

Not long after he delivered the paper, Professor Werthner died, and the club published the paper as a tribute to him.

"On the first day of April, 1796, a score of men, women, and children jumped out of a flat boat that had landed near the mouth of the Mad River. They had come up from Cincinnati to find the new town, called Dayton, and were worn and tired out by the tedious and severe ten-day trip in dreary, wet March weather.

"They scrambled up the bank, hoping to find shelter and warmth in a roomy log cabin where they might eat and rest in comfort. But no cabin, not even a clearing, was to be seen; only a dark and primeval forest, such as would naturally flourish in the fine bottom land along the river. Most of the trees, many of huge proportions, were still in the grip of winter, bare of foliage and uninviting in their nakedness. Here and there, however, along the river, a red maple had sent out clusters of blood red flowers, a promise of spring to come; great old cottonwoods had also hung out their waving, chenille-like tassels of blossoms, while on the white-armed sycamores, bathing their roots in the rushing waters of the Miami, there still dangled the conspicuous seed-balls that had hung on to their twigs all winter.

"None of these things interested the newcomers. They wanted to find Dayton.

"Suddenly, little nine-year-old Mary Van Cleve, the first white girl to step on Dayton soil, called out, 'Here's a blazed tree. Come see what is written on it.'

"Benjamin Van Cleve, a young man of 23, Mary's brother, called to her not to go into the woods alone, remembering that five years before, their father had been killed from ambush by Indians in Kentucky. When he came up to read the scrawl on the blazed tree, 'St. Clair,' he took from his pocket a copy of the Dayton plat and found that St. Clair was the name of the first street running south from the river in the eastern part of the survey.

"Following down the river the group came to the other blazed tree rows running north and south; 'Jefferson,' and still others marked 'Main,' 'Ludlow,' and the last 'Wilkinson.'

"Four days later the first overland party, under Colonel Newcom, arrived, having been two weeks en route from Cincinnati, and a few days later a third party made its appearance."

A plaque in Van Cleve Park commemorates this event. ▪

Muskrat Mystery: One for Sure, and Maybe Two

APRIL 4, 1984

As the river recedes slowly back to normal after the high water of late March, a small island emerges between Salem Avenue and Third Street. Later, the island just becomes part of the flood plain on the east side of the river during normal flow.

It was during the island stage that over 50 ring-billed gulls alighted one evening to fish and spend the night. We've had a number of gulls around all winter, but these were migrants. They came in high from the southwest as if they had been following the flyway of the Miami River like a road map. One by one they peeled off and spiraled downward to land on this small plot of wet ground.

The next day they were still there, but fewer in number. A huge great blue heron took off from the same island, circling nine times to gain altitude, and then made a B-line northward, keeping within visual distance of the Great Miami. This 3½ foot tall bird with 70-inch wingspan might be heading for the large heronry located upstream in Miami County, or it may end up in southern Canada.

Along the riverbanks male redwing blackbirds that have been here since early February are still friendly enough to be singing from the same tree. Just wait until the females arrive and this will all change. Females follow the males in northward migration flight by several weeks.

Male cardinals, song sparrows and robins add to the early spring scene.

Along the west bank the bikeway has nearly emerged from the floodwaters. A lot of debris, mostly logs and small limbs, are deposited, awaiting the Conservancy District cleanup crew. Near the Salem Avenue Bridge the bikeway is lower and still under water.

It was here that a brownish hump resembling a discarded wig seemed worthy of a look through 8x36 binoculars, especially after it appeared to move. Seeing the object magnified eight times provided positive identification of a beautiful muskrat chewing on a piece of vegetation.

This confirmed a sighting of tracks in the snow at almost the same location on New Year's Day. Then, the tracks led across the ice to the open water near the center of the river and disappeared.

This also confirmed a winter sighting reported to me by Mike McDonough. One set of tracks, two muskrats reported at different times, not enough evidence to say if more than one muskrat is here.

This was a fine specimen, feeding and playing around the water's edge.

A muskrat is smaller than a beaver. Its vertically flattened tail acts as a rudder and the slightly webbed hind feet are propellers.

Swimming at top speed, which is about two to three miles per hour, the muskrat makes no headway against the swift current. He dives, and after three or four minutes, surfaces 25 feet upstream. Muskrats can stay under water over 15 minutes, and travel quite a distance before coming up for air. Sight, smell, and hearing are poor, but their sense of direction is excellent.

Muskrats eat practically everything—including poison ivy. They like aquatic plants including cattail, arrowhead and sedges. The latter two can be found along the downtown river floodplain. Clams, mussels, crayfish, snails and dead or dying fish are devoured, when available. Our river can provide all of these muskrat delicacies, and maybe a population of these neat little furbearers will establish here. ▪

Swallows Return: Big Move Back to Nesting Areas Has Begun

APRIL 7, 1993

San Juan, Capistrano, in southern California, is where the swallows always return.

But it has nothing over downtown Dayton—our swallows have returned, too. On March 30 at about 12:30 p.m., I saw six tree swallows flying over the Great Miami River, circling and swooping—appearing to feed on flying insects.

The temperature was in the mid-60s, warm enough for insects and a great day for birds to migrate.

According to *Birds of Dayton*, the average arrival date for tree swallows is Saturday, and the earliest ever recorded for this species in the Miami Valley is February 13, 1965.

Of the five species of swallows seen here, the tree swallow leads the pack during spring migration.

Coming next should be our very own summer resident that nests under the bridge over Wolf Creek at Edwin C. Moses Boulevard, the northern rough-winged swallow.

Just think, wherever you live, there is migration happening over your house at this very minute. There are birds leaving wintering grounds heading for nesting grounds.

Birds are flying at various altitudes, dealing with various weather patterns, covering varying distances, and flying at all times of the day or night.

In *The Country Journal Book of Birding*, Alan Pistorius writes "…if you hung a tiny flashlight on every migrating

North American bird (during spring migration) and assembled a composite time-exposure photograph of the continent, the light streams would be found to crisscross the whole continent (the Rocky Mountain chain would likely remain fairly dark), with considerable tracery evident over both oceans as well. The migratory show is everywhere."

"Well and good," you say. "If migration is going on right over my head, why haven't I seen it?"

You probably haven't looked! Granted, much migration goes on at night with thousands of tiny critters winging it, navigating by the stars or by magnetic fields and coming down to rest and feed during the day.

The large flocks of red-winged blackbirds and tree swallows, both social migrants that fly by day, are probably the best place to start identifying the migratory movement. Migratory flocks of tree swallows sometimes number in the thousands.

The swallows over the Great Miami River were easy to iden-tify—deep bluish-green above, snow-white beneath. Tiny birds, about 5 ½ inches long, often described as having "fluid flight."

Later that day, about 6:30 p.m., I was walking along a ridge trail at Englewood Reserve in a large open meadow near the Stillwater River.

I was not too surprised to hear the liquid twittering sound of tree swallows checking out the bluebird nesting boxes. ▪

Please Say It, Don't Spray It

APRIL 13, 1983

"Sweet William" may reside somewhere near the Oregon District—probably ambled in off U.S. 35's grassy berm. Who knows? But the smell was unmistakable as we walked down Fifth Street to get a chocolate chocolate chip ice cream cone at Tolliver's.

Mephitis, in all objectivity, is a beautiful black and white animal known commonly as a striped skunk, sometimes called a polecat.

Mephitis, literally translated, means "bad odor." By human standards this animal is offensive because it has a defense mechanism that irritates our olfactory receptors and we tend to reject it as an undesirable cohabitant.

De-scented skunks make affectionate cuddly pets whose household antics rival those of the revered family cat.

For you chemists, the musk is a sulfur-alcohol mixed with other sulfur compounds. In addition to being malodorous, the substance is highly acidic and produces an acute burning sensation when directed into the eyes.

Skunks are common in Montgomery County, but obviously not all that common in downtown Dayton. They are nocturnal animals that seldom wander out during the day. They are classified as carnivores, but in addition to eating flesh, they also indulge themselves in berries, nuts, carrion, grasses, garbage, leaves and insects. They love to prey on honeybees and eat dead bees around the outside of the hive as well as live bees as they emerge from the colony. Skunks are apparently impervious to bee stings.

It is difficult to tell a male skunk from a female. Breeding activity starts around February and continues through late March. The gestation period is 60 to 65 days and each mother will produce about five pink-skinned, blind newborn skunks. They use dens, usually in the ground or sometimes in old houses.

Their fur is thick and glossy and is often used in fur trims. However, according to the Ohio Division of Wildlife, there is no market for skunk pelts currently.

If you meet a skunk (four-legged variety) and it raises its tail and taps its front feet impatiently, watch out! You are about to be sprayed, and the musk is hard to wash out of clothing. ▪

Hibiscus Blooms Along Bikeway Inspire Artist to Capture Scene

APRIL 13, 1988

Walking along the Miami River Corridor bikeway, Ave Cassel Barr was inspired by beautiful large hibiscus blooms on some shrubs that grace the landscape at Wolf Creek, near the ornate old Sunrise Bridge.

"I was familiar with hibiscus because my parents live in Florida and have them, but nothing like this," she said. "These blooms were absolutely beautiful and large."

From this inspiration came a painting called "Hibiscus at Wolf Creek," that captures the magic of this beautiful ornamental shrub with its large, white, floppy petals and sensuous red center that has protruding stamens and pistil, the reproductive part of the shrub.

"I encountered a lot of difficulty in painting the blooms," Barr said. The wind was blowing so much that I was painting a continuously moving subject. I am glad the petals didn't blow off."

"Hibiscus at Wolf Creek" was originally painted for entry in the *Dayton by Daytonians* show at the Lazarus Second Floor Gallery.

"I should tell you," Barr said, "that the entry was not accepted. I guess they wanted more architectural type pieces and not flowers."

The painting has two large hibiscus blooms in the foreground with a misty wide-angle panorama of Dayton's city skyline in the background.

"Hibiscus at Wolf Creek" now hangs in the Mutters' "great room" because it portrays a favorite downtown scene where we walk a lot and the pastels just match our new wallpaper.

I asked Ave Barr how she became interested in art. "My mother and dad were both talented," she said. "I was always interested in art. I assumed as a youngster that if I could draw, anyone could do it. It came so easily.

"I didn't take art at all seriously and got a degree in secondary education at Cedar Creek College in Allentown, Pa.

"Instead of teaching, I got married and stayed home to take care of my kids. My husband, Cliff, was then dean of Arts and Sciences at Defiance College in northern Ohio. I decided to take some art courses. A prerequisite course in color and design seemed unnecessary. Knowing the dean, I thought I might just get the course waived. Then I changed my mind and decided to take it."

Barr continued, "This basic course in color composition and unity was taught by a dynamic woman who greatly influenced my decision to take a serious look at art."

Her mentor challenged her. "Have you considered going on in art?"

Barr's reply: "I started painting then and there."

"In my junior year I exhibited at an art show for the first time," she said. "It was a piece formulated from a basic technique called mono-print. You paint on a piece of plexiglass and while the piece is still wet, flip it over and press the painted side firmly into a piece of 100 percent rag paper. After many tries, I got one I liked. I called it "City People."

She explained that the mono-print gave the impression of rapid movement and the void, non-descript areas represented the nameless-faceless crowd of city people.

"As a basically rural person," she said, "I had grown up in a

Girl Scout camp. This was my impression of city people."

Barr is now a professional artist and her husband, Cliff, is dean of Arts and Sciences at Sinclair Community College. The Barrs are now city people themselves, and live downtown in Cooper Place. ▪

New Neighbors

Our Naturalist Says to Watch for a New Treat—
For the First Time Ever House Finches, Who Do
Well in Residential Areas, Appear Downtown

APRIL 24, 1985

*"April is the cruelest month, breeding lilacs out of the dead land,
mixing memory and desire, stirring dull roots with spring rain."*

THOMAS STEARNS ELIOT

April spawns excitement in the natural world. Here are some things to look for in our downtown green spaces.

For the first time ever, house finches have appeared downtown. Not to be confused with house sparrows, these are distinctly different birds, although they have the same habitats.

The male finch is just a bit smaller than the house sparrow, with a bright red throat, a red stripe above the eye and a reddish rump patch. The brown female has stripes on the breast and sides, and a bland face pattern.

Up until 1940, these birds were residents of the eastern part of the country. That year they were released in southeastern New York, and a population explosion followed. By 1980, they had spread west as far as Missouri, south to Georgia and north to southern Canada. House finches were not seen in the Miami Valley until 1973.

The first evidence of nesting locally was in 1981. They are now becoming commonplace. They will be competitive with our resident house sparrows because they do well in residential areas.

House finches nest on branches of trees, old walls, and on raised ledges. They will use the old nests of other birds.

The female builds the nest, a cup-like design of fine grass, leaves, rootlets, string, wool and feathers. She lays four to six smooth, glossy, pale blue eggs and incubates them for 12-14 days.

After all this work by the female, the male finally pitches in and helps feed the newly hatched youngsters.

In 16 days, they are on their own, but the parent birds are not affected by the empty-nest syndrome. They are busy preparing for a second brood, or even a third. No wonder the population is exploding.

• • • • •

Watch Dave Hall Plaza Park behind Stouffer's Dayton Plaza for mallard duck activity. Mike McDonough, who last year discovered a hen mallard with downy ducklings leaving the park and heading for the river by going west on Fourth Street, reported seeing a pair in the park recently.

• • • • •

Male red-winged blackbirds have been here since February. They now have a reason to sit in trees, spread their wings and sing "konk-la-ree." The females are back. They will be nesting in low hedges in downtown parks adjacent to the Miami River.

• • • • •

Speedwells, purple henbit, dark and light blue violets, dandelion, chickweed, and creeping charley comprise most of the early spring wildflowers downtown. Tree flowers are often overlooked because the plant is so large and the flower so small. They offer color, texture and excitement to the still-drab spring landscape. ▪

Plant's 'Beauty' Stifles Other Spring Blooms

APRIL 26, 1995

Dave Barry (*Dayton Daily News*, Lifestyle Section) is not the only columnist to have "alert readers."

An alert reader of the *Downtowner* called me to tell me she had seen the most beautiful "carpet" of yellow and green plants along the banks of the Stillwater River near DeWeese Parkway.

"I think these flowers were marsh marigolds. They were just lovely. They were on the flood plain near the river," the alert reader said.

"Did you count the petals?" I asked.

"Heavens, no," the alert reader replied. I barely had time to look as I rode by on my bike, but they certainly looked like shiny yellow buttercup-like flowers to me."

The plant, lesser celandine, is indeed beautiful as it forms a solid mat of green with its heart-shaped, bluntly toothed leaves and its buttercup, waxy shining petals. It is easily mistaken for marsh and fen oriented marsh marigold. Both are members of the fascinating buttercup family and both bloom in early April in the Miami Valley.

The family name in Latin is Ranunculaceae. The genus name of both plants is Ranunculus. This means little frog, alluding to the wetlands-loving character of many of the family members.

I enjoy the Latin names because they convey the impressions the early botanists had of the plant they were naming.

Lesser celandine is Ranunuculus ficaria meaning "little fig" in reference to the tiny tuber from which it grows and spreads like crazy.

Marsh marigold is most often seen in really wet, marshy places. Its stunning yellow flower parts are called sepals while the equally stunning yellow flower parts of lesser celandine are called petals.

You have to be a botanist to know the difference, so this is of little help to most of us. Lesser celandine likes moist places but may be seen in drier upland sites.

The great big difference is that the lesser celandine, the plant you will see on DeWeese Parkway and on down into the downtown stretch of the Great Miami River, has its leaves coming out of the base of the plant only.

Marsh marigold is a native wildflower, while lesser celandine is an escape from local gardens.

True, beauty is in the eye of the beholder and while one beholder may look at the solid mat of lesser celandine and marvel at its aesthetic presence, I look at it with disgust.

My bias is to see it as an aggressive invader with a spreading tendency that prevents other wildflowers like bloodroot, toothwort, twinleaf and other spring beauties from existing. Wherever it has spread, lesser celandine is completely dominant over any other plant life.

Also along the flood plain of the Great Miami River downtown, you may see cabbage butterflies, mourning cloak and red admiral butterflies—and at night many species of moths.

Mourning cloaks are larger, very attractive butterflies with brownish-maroon wings with yellow borders. They spend the winter, as adults, hibernating in crevices of dead trees or in rocks. They may be seen flying on warm days any month of the year. They feed on tree sap.

Red admirals likewise stay the winter as adults and you may see them flying early in the spring. They like the sap of stinging nettles, false nettles, and willows.

Cabbage butterflies are migrants. I don't know if these early flying cabbage butterflies are returning from a wintering place or if there is an early hatch. If you judge by their name that they feed on cabbage and other vegetables, you are correct. Agricultural producers consider them pests. ▪

May to Bring Flowers, Birds' Songs, Many Metamorphoses

MAY 6, 1992

Oh month of flowering, month of metamorphoses,
May without cloud and June that was stabbed,
I shall never forget the lilac and the roses,
Nor those whom spring has kept in its folds.

LOUIS ARAGON, 1897-1982

Welcome to May, a change from the flowers of April, an introduction to the early summer, a great month to enjoy nature to its fullest. More songbirds will be heard this month, more wildflowers may be seen and more seeds will be planted in fields and gardens, in urban window boxes and on deck planters than during any other month.

Watch for May's full moon on Saturday, the 16th.

It is appropriately called the Flower Moon, or Moon of Flowers. In his book *Moods of Ohio Moons* (Kent State University Press, 1991), Merrill Gilfillan wrote: A popular Indian pictograph for May shows a singing bird perched on the handle of an Indian planting stick, a combination of two moons, the Song Moon and the Planting Moon.

When you go outside on your break or for lunch this month, there will be a lot to observe. If you don't see anything of interest at ground level, you can always scan the heavens for interesting cloud formations and approaching storms. If this pursuit interests you, there are a couple of books that help you understand what is going on up there, *Storms—Their Origins and Effects* (Golden Press, 1969), and *A Field Guide to the Atmosphere* (Houghton-Mifflin Co., 1981).

I was driving downtown last week on a cold and rainy day. Visibility was low because of the low-lying stratus clouds just a few hundred feet above the city. Suddenly raindrops began to bounce off the hood and the windshield—sleet was falling. Sleet forms when rain from a higher pocket of warm air falls through a layer of freezing air.

Raindrops become freezing rain that will stick to trees and wires if the ground temperature is below freezing. Or, if the frozen drops pass through more freezing air, they form tiny ice pellets—or true sleet—and begin falling to the earth.

A characteristic of sleet is the bouncing effect upon hitting a hard surface.

You are more likely to see hail this time of year and later in the summer. Often reported to be the size of golf balls, there have been hailstones as large as a human fist. Hailstones usually form in thunderheads about 20,000-22,000 feet high.

They start as frozen rain, but instead of falling, they are swept upward by violent updrafts in the thunderhead. Here they are super-cooled and pick up layers of ice. As they become heavy with added layers of ice, they begin to fall to the earth's surface.

If you can run out and gather some hailstones after they have fallen, cut one in half. It will have a layered appearance like an onion.

Obviously, hail can be hazardous to humans, crops and windows. Large hailstones can seriously damage the paint on your car, especially if you are driving at a high rate of speed.

Sleet on the ground is hazardous only if the ground temperatures are low and it sticks to sidewalks and streets.

Other exciting phenomena are there for the watching. Some require an exercise in caution—e.g. tornadoes and lightning.

A good rule of thumb, when you are out in the early stages of a thunderstorm and when lightning is crackling nearby, may help you decide when to take cover. I use this often when canoeing or hiking to judge how close a storm may be, and whether it is approaching or moving away from my location.

Simply begin counting seconds, one thousand one, one thousand two—immediately after a lightning flash. Stop counting when you hear the crack of thunder caused by the bolt of lightning. Since light and sound travel at different rates of speed—you can get a fairly accurate ETA (estimated time of arrival) for the storm.

After counting seconds, divide by five to determine the number of miles the storm is from you. A 15-second count would place the storm three miles away. If shorter, it is moving in your direction. Don't depend on one count. Do several. ▪

A Hike at Lunch May
Turnip Things to Munch

MAY 18, 1983

Dave Hall Plaza by Stouffer's is a delight to stroll through on
your noon lunch break.

Flowering trees and plants abound to pique your aesthetic
sensibilities. But ask your self the question: "Is there anything
here I can eat?"

How about a wild salad or a rich full-bodied coffee substitute? Perhaps a delicate sweet wine could be garnered from the
offerings at the Plaza.

Ridiculous you say.

Not so if you follow these two simple rules:

1. Get there before the City Parks and Recreation
   Department maintenance crew does, and

2. Stick to dandelions and one or two other plants.

I browsed through the Plaza a few days ago before any weed-
ing had been done. This is the best time to observe the weeds,
defined as plants out of place. But weeds really indicate the early
invading natural plants that appear on open soil to fill a niche
where nothing else is growing.

Dandelions, of course, were here, in the lawn and in the beds,
and if you need an additional source for your wild food lunch,
go to the little triangle just east of the Dayton Convention and
Exhibition Center parking garage across from the Greyhound
Bus Station and you'll find solid dandelions.

The plant is grossly maligned and despised by urban and suburban lawn tenders. It gets dug, sprayed, mowed, chopped and pulled by its roots, but seldom gathered as a delicious edible herb.

The dandelion alone rivals the finest prepared mushrooms. Fresh dandelion blossoms moistened, dipped in seasoned flour and fried in butter are truly a treat.

The fresh blossoms, when properly prepared and fermented, make a deliciously delicate white wine.

The roots may be dug, dried and ground into a coarse powder that makes a somewhat bitter but acceptable coffee substitute.

One plant I observed that you do not want to try to use in your noontime salad or to garnish your next pot roast is poison hemlock. I saw only one plant, and it is probably windblown. It is common all over Montgomery County, and I was not surprised to see it.

It is in the carrot family and has attractive lacy leaves like Queen Anne's Lace, also a member of the carrot family. The features to look for are purple flecks on the smooth stem of the poison hemlock plant.

The so-called weeds, the very plants selected for destruction by the maintenance crew so the planted species will look better, tell an exciting story. The story is of the maverick seeds that have found their way into the green oasis in downtown Dayton.

Some of the seeds were probably in the topsoil hauled in and carefully graded to make the attractive topography of this unique green space. Others came in on the wind, and still others have been carried in by birds and deposited in their droppings.

Natural succession is at work here just the same as at Taylorsville Reserve or the Smoky Mountains National Park or in your garden.

Now for the wild food foray. Wild garlic is growing in profusion. It looks like a cross between garden-variety green onions and the little herb called chives. Wild garlic smells and tastes like garlic and can be used (sparingly, because it's strong) in salads, or cut and dried like chives and sprinkled on meat.

Garlic mustard appears in the Plaza beds, but I saw only two plants. Unlike the long tubular leaves of wild garlic, the leaves of garlic mustard are round and flat.

Crush the leaf and smell it or taste the tip of a broken stem and you immediately perceive the mixed flavor of garlic and mustard. Obviously the taxonomist who originally described and named the plant did just that. ▪

On a Clear Day You Can't See the Buckeye Trees in Cooper Park

JUNE 1, 1983

From the tenth floor up, if you're in the Kettering Tower on the east side of the building, you have a commanding view of Cooper Park.

A reader whose office is located in the tower called the other day to suggest I write about the buckeye trees in the little 3.2 acre park adjacent to the Dayton-Montgomery County Public Library.

I would be glad to oblige, but there are no buckeye trees in Cooper Park. Instead, there are two large horse chestnut trees that have just completed bearing their showy masses of white flowers for this spring. They resemble buckeyes very much. The horse chestnut is a native of southeastern Europe but is widely planted in the United States. In fact, it has escaped to the northeast and is doing well on its own. It is a cousin to our state tree, the Ohio buckeye.

If you follow Latin names, they both are from the genus "Aesculus." Visibly, the trees look almost identical except for the usual number of leaflets on each leaf. The buckeye has five palmately compound (like fingers from the palm of your hand) leaflets and the horse chestnut has seven. Another difference is flower color. The buckeye tree sports pale, greenish-yellow flowers; the horse chestnut, snowy white. The fruits (seeds) are similar in appearance and poisonous to people. Watch for them in September and early October.

The horse chestnut is easily propagated from seed and is tolerant of city conditions. Turks reportedly used the shiny brown seeds to concoct a remedy to give to horses suffering from a cough, hence the name.

Observers from the Kettering Tower probably noticed these large horse chestnut trees during the peak of their bloom. Other trees worth watching in Cooper Park are the walnut, gingko, linden, and the maple. Years ago, the park was covered in American elms, long since victims of the infamous Dutch elm disease.

Things not so easily seen but observed at ground level include gray squirrels, Kentucky warblers, yellow-bellied sapsuckers (yes, they're real), crows, and white-throated sparrows. ▪

Swarm of Locusts "Plague" City with Shade, Beauty

JUNE 19, 1985

It's hard not to talk about downtown trees.

Visually, they contribute so much to the cityscape, and with their increasing numbers, the center city is a nice place to be.

Walking north on the east side of Main Street past Market Square you can see the patriarch of downtown Moraine locusts. This tree shades much of the walk into the mall that leads to the Lebanese Deli and the former Admiral Benbow Inn.

Our destination was the pre-opening party at Vic Cassano's newest pizza and sub restaurant at 116 N. Main Street, but spotting some more Moraine locusts, we detoured westward on Third Street, walking by the Old Courthouse and the Dayton Power & Light Company Building.

Turning north on Ludlow Street to Second Street, there are more of these trees with the fine textured foliage. East on Second Street along the sidewalk by Elder-Beerman there are more of these thornless locust trees.

Bob Siebenthaler, president of the Siebenthaler Company, knows a great deal about these trees because the family patented and developed the variety.

"This was the first tree to be patented in the United States and developed here," Siebernthaler said. "It was in 1948-49. The prototypical tree was found at Benson and Audry Place, a couple blocks south of Good Samaritan Hospital."

The Moraine locust is a patented clone taken from the original male tree and is not only thornless, but bears no pods to clutter urban streets. The common honey locust (Gleditsia tricanthos) is the parent of this thornless variety. Unlike the thornless "Inermis" variety, the honey locust has strong, straight, brown, branched, shiny, sharp thorns four to six inches long. It produces a long fruit in the shape of a pod, eight to ten inches long. These pods, when ripe in the early autumn, contain a sweet pulp surrounding the hard brown seeds. Some attribute the "honey" in the locust to this sweet fruit.

"The trees are virtually disease resistant," Siebenthaler said. "In downtown Chicago the very center of the city is planted with Moraine locusts because of their ability to survive in an urban environment."

The Siebenthalers' primary impetus to develop the thornless, podless locust was a need to find a species to replace the rapidly dying American elm.

Nurserymen in the 1930s searched the woods for the "Inermis," the thornless variety from which they made cuttings in order to grow their stock in trade. Nursery stock had to be propagated asexually, which is the long, slow process of rootings, cuttings and caring for them until they are large enough to plant.

It was not until the late '40s or '50s that the Siebenthaler nursery began mass production of the species.

"Another reason this makes a good street tree," Siebenthaler explained, "is that the leaves are so small that at leaf fall little street maintenance is required. One good rain and they disappear into the storm drain. Our trees are now distributed coast to coast."

A few weeks ago, in Seattle, I walked along tree-lined streets and saw Moraine locusts. It was great to say, "These trees were originally developed in Dayton." ▪

Drawing Birds Offers Downtown Artist an Escape from Frustration

JUNE 22, 1988

"What we see is not as important as how we perceive what we see," says Phillip Rusten, author of *A Way of Seeing*, a book about his visual philosophy.

Although Rusten is a photographer of nature, his guiding principles are similar to those of many artists who produce visual images that capture the excitement of the natural world in a form shared by others.

"Art bares the soul of the artist," Rusten adds. "What I want my pictures to reveal is a sense of joy at being alive and about in this marvelous world."

Gwen Smith, a downtowner living in the Park Layne apartments, is an aspiring artist who began doing pen and ink sketches while in high school.

She, like Rusten, is imbued with the marvels of the natural world.

"To me, she says, "art is a personal satisfier, a great way to relieve stress after a hard day at work." She is an associate administrator in human resources at the divisional personnel department at Delco Moraine.

"I like the outdoors and nature because of the freedom it gives me," she said.

She likes most of all to study birds, paying attention to detail.

"The minute I focus my attention on the shape, form and color of a bird, the way the wings look, how the feathers are attached, and the intricate design of the feathers, I can just feel the frustration leaving my body. I am concentrating on something beyond myself."

Smith was raised in Winchester, Kentucky, a few miles east of Lexington. She attributes her early interest in nature to summertime visits to her grandparents in the country.

Stimulated by the experience, that is also when she began to draw birds.

"During boredom time," she said, "I would do sketches of birds. I did one of an owl that was pretty good. At least that is what my friends tell me."

Smith continued, "One year we studied Ray Harm, the famous Kentucky wildlife artist. He was a real source of inspiration. I also read *Audubon Magazine* and *National Geographic* and got a lot of ideas from them."

Talking about her dream agenda, she says, "I want to have the time to paint different kinds of birds. Birds have character and strength. To me, eagles have immense power and I hope someday to be able to paint one. I also want to do parrots, peacocks and other exotic birds. Someday I may do an exhibit and if am lucky, sell some art."

She plans to use pen and ink, pastels, charcoal, acrylics and tempera as media to express her interest in birds.

Satisfaction comes to Gwen Smith in seeing art as it is created.

"Just seeing the picture coming together on paper or canvas," she says, "and seeing it come to life and saying 'Gosh, this came from my hand.' That's a personal satisfier."

One of the most satisfying efforts to date is a pair of mallards done in charcoal then lightly covered with pastels.

She jogs and bikes a lot along the River Corridor Bikeway and gets ideas for her favorite art subjects there. ▪

Hitchhikers: Alien Life Forms Travel with Humans, Colonize

JUNE 25, 1986

When human beings became mobile and started spreading their kind around the planet, they took a lot of hitchhiking organisms along with them.

Plants and animals of various geographical localities have been carried around the globe, unwittingly, in packs of seed shipped to pioneer settlers of new lands, or, in the case of starlings, sold and delivered to the colonies because Eugene Schieffelin, an avid fan of Shakespeare, believed that Americans should experience every bird mentioned in Shakespeare's plays.

The majority of the plants in downtown vacant lots and street-side crannies are wayside plants from Europe—the teasel, daisy, mullein, day lily, chicory and dandelion, to name just a few.

A house mouse, a starling and an English sparrow find London little different than New York City or Dayton. Likewise, the alien plants that follow humans across the ocean.

The first recorded location for many foreign plants and animals was a seaport or railroad track. Whatever our travel mode, aliens are sure to travel, and outer space is no exception.

When Pete Conrad, captain of the Apollo 12 mission, spoke at Sinclair Community College recently, he related a fascinating story of bacterium that survived 33 months on the moon. Temperatures ranged from –250 degrees to +250 degrees Fahrenheit. It is not a "life-friendly" environment. It seems the camera left by Neil Armstrong and retrieved two years and nine months later by Pete Conrad contained a single bacterium in the insulation packed around the camera's parts.

Mystified technicians and scientists theorized and speculated on the origin of this little fellow until a packing technician remembered sneezing into the insulation as it was being fitted into the camera before the first moon flight.

The microscopic life form had hitched a ride into outer space and back.

It failed to colonize the moon, as ragweed and pigeons did when brought to this continent from Europe, but it did survive. One might imagine that, in a short time, Canada thistles and cockle burrs, as well as bacteria, might establish on a space station or even planets we visit where the environment is right.

One of the most recent aliens to visit downtown Dayton is the nodding thistle. A few years ago it was a rare plant around Montgomery County. Now it is becoming a pest, but a beautiful pest, I might add.

You are immediately attracted to its large reddish purple flower head, often nodding or drooping as it ages. Purple bracts appear as a collar of lance-like "petals" just below the flower.

Thistles belong to the composite, or daisy family. This is the largest family of flowering plants in the world, and probably the most advanced plants to appear. The flower head is a cluster of many small flowers, each taking advantage of one sturdy prickly stem and stiff spiny leaves. This makes for production of many seeds, thus assuring the survival of the plant. It blooms from June to early July and possibly later in our area.

The seeds, typical of all thistles, are equipped with long, soft hairs that aid in the wind-borne distribution of the plant.

Another attractive "weed" to look for right now is purple

loosestrife. The slender petaled flowers are tinged with magenta. Several plants about three feet tall are in full bloom along the east bank of the Great Miami River just downstream from the Monument Street Bridge. ▪

Wolf Creek Proves to be Natural Hub in Dayton, Beyond

JUNE 27, 1990

At the mouth of Wolf Creek its clear water flows into the Great Miami River. There is always activity here.

People are fishing. There are runners, walkers and bikers, one or two, sometimes hundreds crossing Wolf Creek on the low water span that is the Miami River Corridor Bikeway.

I have covered much of the Wolf Creek corridor from the Miami River to Brookville and find it a fascinating stream. Downtown at the Third Street Bridge we have, for the past eight years, observed rare yellow-crowned night herons and a few black-crowned night herons feeding in the gravelly shallows below the low dam. They are often accompanied by the sounds of bullfrogs. All are active at night.

Ospreys, the graceful fish hawks, are often seen hunting here during migration, and great blue herons and kingfishers frequent this productive river "cafeteria."

Moving upstream, under the Edwin C. Moses Bridge, Wolf Creek is contained by steep, grassy banks. The north side bank is a glacial moraine and the south side bank is a levee, constructed for flood control purposes. At the Summit Street Bridge, where the old Pennsylvania Railroad crossed the creek, the banks begin to look more natural, and the creek meanders more. It is in this wooded area that some of the yellow and black-crowned night herons nest.

This is also the vicinity of the old Dayton Tire and Rubber Company plant where PCBs were flushed into Wolf Creek a couple years ago. PCBs are polychlorinated biphenyls, toxic chemicals found in old electric transformers. Here we have observed bass, suckers, bluegills, carp, a variety of smaller fish, Canada geese with goslings and mallard ducks with ducklings.

Moving upstream, Wesleyan Road Park features the Wesleyan Road Nature Center with several acres of natural area, and just west of Gettysburg is Hickorydale Park.

In Trotwood, the north branch of Wolf Creek goes in a northerly direction, draining the area around Clayton, and the south branch moves northwest to its headwaters in the rich farmlands around Brookville.

If we were hiking up Wolf Creek from Dayton, the destination would be Sycamore State Park, 2200 acres of public land situated between Trotwood and Brookville offering unlimited recreation and habitat development potential. Think of the prospect of linking downtown Dayton to Sycamore State Park via a bikeway or hiking trail and developing a permanent green corridor along Wolf Creek.

Many areas in the United States are taking this progressive approach to solving open space problems by establishing greenways along the rivers and utilizing old railroad rights of way for hiking and biking trails.

Keith Hay, director of Greenways for America is with the Conservation Fund in Arlington, Virginia. I met Hay in San Francisco in January at a parks symposium on planning river corridors. Hay says, "Americans like to be on the move; we are not a people to go to a park and sit."

His comment is borne out when it shows in the President's Commission on Open Space Report that walking is the No. 1 outdoor recreation in the United States. Hay also made a point that, within the rapidly escalating price of land, it is difficult to set aside large blocks of parkland and more realistic to plan for greenways and corridors. ▪

Falcon Patrol Helps Keep Fledgling Flier Afloat

JULY 7, 1993

In spite of the loss of one falcon chick, the presence of the birds downtown has been a valuable educational experience—a graduate-level course in the life history of falcons.

Thousands of downtowners and Miami Valley residents have benefited from first-hand observation or from the excellent media coverage of the biological processes so essential to the life—and death—of wild things.

On June 25, the first of the two chicks fledged. It had been flapping vigorously and jumping up on the ledge in the nest on the west side of the old Lazarus building, but not quite confident enough to make the first leap into space. At 7:30 p.m., a gust of wind solved that problem and the young falcon no longer had a choice, she was airborne.

Her first flight was west on Second Street, where she attempted to land on the Hulman Building. She tried to grasp a ledge where none existed, then fluttered none too gracefully down to street level.

"A bird in the street" is one of the greatest concerns wildlife managers have of new fledglings in an urban setting—and this is the reason for the Falcon Patrol, the group of volunteers that pledged to try to protect the young birds if they get into trouble or are injured in any way.

June 25 was the first day of the Falcon Watch Patrol. Earlier that afternoon my wife, Priscilla, had arrived from a two-week trip to Russia and Eastern Europe. I greeted her with an announcement that we had signed up for a 6 to 9 p.m. watch with the Falcon Patrol.

At 6 p.m. we checked out a two-way radio provided by the Ohio Division of Wildlife, at Mead Security headquarters and proceeded to rendezvous with three other volunteers who were already on the purple level of the Nationwide Parking Garage, the best location to observe young chicks on the nest.

We introduced ourselves to Tom Hanselman, Joe Tarkany and Cindy Sunnycalb. I used to work with Hanselman's brother when he was an environmental planner for the Miami Valley Regional Planning Commission. Sunnycalb, a teacher at Cox Elementary School in Xenia, last year had presented me with a check for the Beaver Creek Wetlands Association from an aluminum recycling project that her class held. It's a small world.

Thirty minutes later we were back to our post at the Nationwide Parking Garage, watching the other chick, when a bird appeared on the rim of the Hulman Building roof. At first we thought it was Rachel, the parent bird.

Wrong!

On close observation, the dark streaked breast and some down on the head meant the chick was not happy with the Hulman Building roof, and soon was airborne for her second journey, this time by choice.

She flew from a much higher perch than the nest box at Lazarus. From the top of the Hulman Building she glided and flapped catty-corner across Second Street and northbound of Wilkinson Street—and with such speed that we lost sight of her.

We grabbed the box, took the elevator down to street level, and started the search. I went back to Mead Security to check out another two-way radio so we could communicate and had just turned it on when I heard Sunnycalb calling "We've found her—she's on the Reibold Building perched on the very top of the building."

That seemed the wrong direction and a long distance for the bird to have traveled. I made a call to Rick Jasper, acting district supervisor for the Wildlife District Five and the person in charge of the falcon projects in Dayton and Cincinnati.

Just as Jasper answered, Sunnycalb came on the two-way with "Correction, the chick in on the Talbott Tower, not the Reibold Building, and she seems to be OK. Still no sign of either parent and it's getting dark."

On the phone, Jasper advised that the bird would probably stay put for the night, but that if did get down to street level again we should try to reach Lazarus Security and get it back in the original nest. This was not necessary, as the bird stayed on the perch on the west rim of the Talbott Tower all night and fared well.

Another player that night was Dayton police officer Dyra Money, of the mounted patrol, doing double duty in a patrol car. She was very helpful in spreading the word through the Dayton police network that a falcon chick was out of the nest and to keep an eye out.

While she was making some entries on her console computer, we pointed out the chick on the Talbott Tower perch and at the same moment, just about 100 chimney swifts were circling the castle-like tower/chimney on the church at First and Wilkinson Streets and were beginning to drop into the chimney to spend the night.

Downtown Dayton is truly a bio-diverse place. ▪

Bullfrogs Enjoy Life Along the Miami

AUGUST 3, 1983

A vibrant, sonorous series of bass notes best paraphrased as "jug-a-rum, jug-a-rum" has been heard on several occasions recently along the Great Miami River—unmistakably the voice of a bullfrog (Lithobates catesbeianus.)

A pleasant surprise, as I was not expecting to hear this big amphibian in the downtown stretch of the Miami.

Bullfrogs are here, and the booming voice of the males signals the time of year when breeding season is in progress. The bullfrog is large and provides us with most of the commercial frog legs sold in supermarkets and restaurants.

It is our largest frog, with its body measuring 3 ½ to 6 inches (record is 8), and it prefers larger bodies of water than do most frogs. The sluggish pools of the Miami are lined along the water's edge with water willow or swamp loosestrife. This attractive plant has essential input into the ecological balance along our river. It provides much needed cover for many aquatic dwellers, including the bullfrog. The plant also has an attractive lavender bloom. Here the frogs are well hidden from sight and so are more often heard than seen.

You will remember from eighth grade biology that amphibians, according to their name, live at least part of their lives in water, and part on land. Bullfrogs are aquatic. They breed, get their food, and hibernate, usually in the same body of water, spending little time on land.

Bullfrogs are the last of the frogs to come out of hibernation in the spring and usually the last to breed in the summer. They lay their eggs at night during late June or July. The egg mass is nearly two feet across and floats near the surface, anchored and half hidden in the plant stems or brush near the water's edge. This mass is a film of jelly, containing 10,000 to 20,000 small eggs.

Unlike most other frogs, bullfrog tadpoles take two years and sometimes even three years to mature. They are huge compared to other tadpoles, sometimes growing to six inches in length.

Several days ago I saw several of these large tadpoles feeding below the small dam where Wolf Creek empties into the Great Miami River. This is proof enough of successful reproduction for bullfrogs in this stretch of the river. Keep in mind that any tadpole over three and one-half inches has to be a bullfrog tadpole; one-year-old bullfrog tadpoles seldom have hind legs. These tadpoles had both front and hind legs, indicating that they've been alive for at least two years, and they may become mature frogs by autumn. Their presence in the Great Miami indicates a fairly high water quality.

These frogs, while easily identified by their size and sound, have some other identifying features worth mentioning. They are plain green above, with a somewhat netlike pattern of grey or brown on a green background below. The males have a wash of yellow on their throats. ▪

Bats Cleaner than People Think; Do Their Best to Rid Downtown of Insects

AUGUST 17, 1988

Bats are in right now.

A great deal is being written on the preservation of bats, as several species are on state and national endangered lists.

The Feb. 28, 1988 issue of *The New Yorker* magazine featured a story on bats. Author Diane Ackerman wrote: "A single small insect-eating bat can eat a thousand insects each night, so these bats are a good investment for a homeowner." Bat Conservation International (B.C.I.) sells "official bat houses" to hang on buildings to emphasize what good citizens bats are.

Bats are common downtown animals. Ackerman, writing from Austin, Tex., said, "At dinner time I head downtown and try the patio of the Four Seasons Hotel, which is on Town Lake, a few blocks from the pink granite capitol and across from the Congress Avenue Bridge. Tucked inside the crevices under the bridge are three-quarters of a million bachelor free-tailed bats. This makes Austin the summer home of the largest urban bat population in the world."

Not to be outdone, downtown Dayton has a good population of bats. You need only to observe, at dusk, in any of the downtown's natural areas, the hungry little mammals reducing the city's population of insects.

Many of you have experienced the appearance of bats at Memorial Hall performances. Last week another enthusiastic caller provided us with a fantastic bat story that took place in the Arcade Rotunda.

"People were craning their necks and pointing toward the top of the Arcade Rotunda," the caller said. "Then another group pointed and I heard someone say 'There it is.' I looked up, and there was a large bat with a 10-inch wingspan, circling near the Arcade turkeys in the glass-domed rotunda. Every ten minutes or so the bat would circle down through Charley's Crab, unobserved by the noontime clientele enjoying their lunch, and then return to its perch in the top of the rotunda.

"At one time the bat swooped down and circled Rinaldo's Bakery, causing a stir among customers. As the bat continued to circle, the wise manager at Charley's opened the door to the kitchen, and the bat flew in and disappeared"

My caller said he became extremely curious, jumped into the glass elevator and went up to Charley's, where he confronted the manager and asked, "What happened to the bat that flew into the kitchen?"

The reply: "I just opened the door to the adjacent building and the bat flew out."

End of the bat story, except to emphasize to those who may be upset at the thought of a bat flying through a kitchen, bats are one of the cleanest animals, including human beings. They spend much time cleaning while hanging upside down. They lick and clean thoroughly every bit of the body and wings that can be reached with their long red tongues. Then, moistening the hind foot, they clean the hair on the back and the top of their heads and spend a lot of time cleaning their valuable ears. Brown bats have been known to spend at least a half hour on their baths. ▪

Milkweed's Bitter Milk Tastes Sweet to Insects, Butterflies

SEPTEMBER 13, 1989

Calling all butterflies of every race
From source unknown but from no special place.
They ever will return to their lives
Because unlike the bees they have no hives.
The milkweed brings up to my very door
The theme of wanton waste in peace and war—
And, yes, although it is a flower that flows
With milk and honey, it is bitter milk as anyone who ever
broke its stem
And dared to taste the wound a little knows
It tastes as if it might be opiate.

From, *Pod of the Milkweed*
ROBERT FROST

The common milkweed is a stout downy plant. Asclepias is the generic, Latin name for Asclepias, the Greek god of medicine. Flower clusters of milkweed vary in subtle shades of dusty rose, lavender, and dull brownish purple. Each flower is unique in its geometry and the broken stem produces a thick milky juice that can substitute for Elmer's glue in a pinch.

A few lone milkweeds stand halfway up the levee bank, spared from the last mowing. As summer wanes, the self-pollinating flowers have developed long, pointed grey-green pods filled with airborne seeds. Come autumn, the pods dry, crack open and disperse their silken load. As nature would have it, each seed is attached to its own feathery parachute, set to travel an unlimited distance with the help of air currents.

Many insects thrive on he juices of these plants despite the bitter taste and somewhat toxic qualities identified by human standards.

Noticing that generous quantities of the upper leaves were missing from some of these plants caused me to carefully search the lower leaves. As expected, colonies of milkweed tiger moth larvae were quietly munching a late summer meal. Upon being discovered, some of the wooly larvae rolled into balls and dropped from the plants, thus displaying an effective defense mechanism.

The black and white larva with long tufts of hair on either end creates the illusion of having two heads, perhaps another way to confuse predators. Soon these larvae will roll into cozy, hairy cocoons to spend the winter, and then next spring, hatch into light brown moths with wings about two inches in width.

Another insect commonly associated with the milkweeds is the monarch butterfly. These large migratory insects spend much of their life cycle on various species of milkweed, hence the name, milkweed butterfly. Its eggs are deposited here and the larvae feed hungrily on the leaves.

The toxic quality of milkweed plays an important role in the life expectancy of the monarch. The larvae retain the toxins picked up from the acrid, white milk, and pass them along to the pupa stage. This chemistry is apparently still present in the adult monarch, making it toxic to any would-be predator.

Lepidopterists, people who study butterflies, have tagged hundreds of monarchs over the last few years. Returns from tagged specimens reveal that our butterflies make their way to Mexico for the winter.

The return flight is made by succeeding generations with "Dayton, Ohio, and vicinity" imprinted in their genes. ▪

October 7 Special for Downtown Naturalist

There are two events I associate with October 7:

- One is October 7, 1966, the birthday of my youngest son, Denis.
- The other is, since October 7, 1982, the migrating chimney swifts have made an annual stopover at the First Unitarian Church on Salem Avenue.

I'm sure the swifts have used the chimney long before 1982, but it was that year that Ken Sinks, administrator of the church, called to tell me "I have just observed a large number of bats flying into the chimney at dusk here at the church." "Bats," I told Ken, "should fly out of the 'cave' at dusk. Let's meet at the church tomorrow evening and see what's going on."

At 7:27 p.m. on October 7, 1982, we watched an estimated 1000 swifts swirl around the huge chimney and drop inside. In the dusky twilight their rapid wing beats, tailless bodies and their habit of clustering together before going to roost, could easily be mistaken for that of small bats.

This year we took Denis and his friend, Melissa, out for a birthday dinner. We stopped at the First Unitarian Church at 7:27 p.m. and watched some 200 birds circling the chimney like a black tornado and then descending for a night's rest before continuing their journey to the rain forests of Peru to winter.

By now they will be gone except for a few stragglers. They have been seen in Dayton as late as November 10, but that is exceptional. The birds' unerring timing keeps pushing them southwest ahead of the early winter squalls. Most important, the autumn movement is to keep up with the supply of insects so essential to their diet.

Swifts spend most of their day in the air, feeding as they travel. Their wide mouths are adapted to making a series of catches of their favorite prey. Their five-inch-long bodies are proportioned well to fit their 12 ½ inch-long wings, making long flights possible.

European swifts seldom land except to nest. They often sleep while soaring.

These birds will have a pleasant winter (summer) some 300-400 miles south of the equator. They will feed, gain maximum weight, and prepare to fly back north, arriving in downtown Dayton in mid-April. They are one of the most common birds seen here in the summer.

It's exciting to watch the communal roosting behavior of swifts during their spring and fall migration.

If you have never had the opportunity, put the date on your calendar a year ahead, find a large chimney, and experience an exhibit of unusual bird behavior. ▪

Starling Behavior
Perfectly Natural

OCTOBER 30, 1991

As October's full moon rose over Building 12 on the Sinclair Community College campus last Wednesday, October 23, the sun was setting in the hazy western sky.

In two directions, east toward the rising moon and west toward the setting sun, starlings swirled overhead in large numbers.

With ample daylight remaining, I walked around the campus observing early evening starling behavior while waiting for my wife, Priscilla.

The low, lollipop-shaped trees—also along the east side of South Perry Street—had shed few leaves and were loaded with starlings. The trees were beautiful with leaves ranging in color from green to orange, dense enough to hide the birds. As I looked and listened from the west side of the street, I got a surreal impression of these colorful trees emitting a cacophony of New-Age music, the various sounds of several hundred starlings. With several loud claps of my hands, the music ceased and the sky above filled with milling, confused birds—including a few mourning doves.

This kind of starling behavior is normal, although my behavior may have been perceived as a bit weird by a couple of people talking near Parking Lot E next to the day care center. Oh well, that's the risk one takes when observing downtown wildlife.

As the birds exploded from this site, the sturdy oaks on the west side of the day care center were now devoid of birds and were left with only deep reddish brown leaves.

I crossed the street to the Milk Marketing facility. Here thick hedges border the well-kept grounds of the plant. Some song sparrows scurried to roost. Washington haws are laden with red fruit, excellent winter robin food for those choosing not to migrate.

In the tall Moraine locust trees between the Milk Marketing paved lot and the old Dayton Metropolitan Housing Association building, more starlings were clustered, singing in the treetops. Upon my approach, they exploded into a swirl and disappeared in the direction of the Great Miami River.

Again, this behavior is normal. It's the thing starlings do this time of year as the various feeding groups gather in early evening just before sunset in large flocks for roosting. It annoys us, but it is normal behavior for them.

Their Latin name, Sturnis vulgaris, means common starling. Their early evening flocking both disturbed and intrigued customers at the Dayton Marriott Hotel the other evening as large flocks descended into the trees at the main entrance.

Starlings did not come to the United States by their own volition; we brought them here. They were introduced in Pennsylvania before 1850, but did not establish.

Later releases were made in Ohio, Massachusetts, New Jersey, New York and Oregon between 1870 and 1900. The only nesting successes from these efforts were from 100 birds introduced in New York City in 1890, and 160 in 1891. So the starlings have been around a century now and are well distributed over the entire United States. The Audubon Christmas Bird Count a few years ago reported more than 8000 starlings seen per hour of count effort.

I enjoy their normal behavior, though I'm sure grounds maintenance crews at Sinclair do not. But this is the result of man manipulating the natural world a hundred years ago. ▪

Shaggy Mane Mushrooms
Taste Wonderful

OCTOBER 31, 1984

This is the eve of All Saints Day, referred to in medieval England as Hallow's Eve and by most of us as Halloween. Around the haunts of most witches and goblins toadstools and slime molds flourish, adding to the mystique of haunted forests and the inhabitants therein.

A real forest can be more exciting and mysterious than a haunted one. It doesn't even have to be a forest. Would you believe a vacant lot in downtown Dayton? No, we don't see any toadstools or witches, but rather a fine display of shaggy mane mushrooms, 20 or so in number.

Now, shaggy manes could fit right into a Halloween setting. They look almost unreal with their tall cylindrical caps covered with shaggy flat scales. The cap is two to four inches tall and the stem is four to eight inches tall.

I discovered these choice edible mushrooms just west of the YMCA on a vacant gravel lot between Monument Street and the Great Miami River. I was leading one of John Walker's "Walk into History" hikes, sponsored by Sinclair Community College, when we happened upon the shaggy manes. They quickly disappeared, as savvy students collected these edibles.

Shaggy manes are one of the most delightful of all edible mushrooms. They should be prepared for the table just as soon as possible after being collected. Just overnight these "Inky Caps," as this family of fungi is known, begin to autodigest.

This means they start to digest themselves as the gills of the mature mushrooms dissolve into a black inky fluid. This is caused by an enzyme that is inactivated by cooking.

However, it has been my experience in cooking shaggy manes that once the deliquescence has started, the flavor decreases.

Recently, I have spotted several other mushrooms around town at Sunrise Park and at Dave Hall Plaza near Stouffer's. Rainy weather has prompted their growth.

Some mushrooms are eminently edible, while others are deadly poisonous. If you are not 100% sure, leave it alone!

The primary function of mushrooms and other fungi in general is not to feed human beings. Quite the contrary, they are decomposers, the silent majority of organisms that are agents of decay.

Can you imagine what it would be like if everything that had ever lived and died were still here? Our life system would have short-circuited long ago. Decay is carried out largely by bacteria, yeasts and molds breaking down dead bodies, plant litter and other wastes, allowing the chemical element in such substances to be released and recycled.

Without decay, the soil would become barren and plant life would be choked off for lack of nutrients. In short, the earth's energy cycle would come to a halt and all life would perish.

Mushrooms are a special kind of fungi. Unlike green plants, fungi lack chlorophyll and must live on organic matter. *Coprinus comatus*, the shaggy mane, is able to live on buried wood and other organic litter anywhere on earth. ∎

Miami River Contains Wealth of Game Fish

NOVEMBER 7, 1984

With deadeye accuracy, the young fisherman casts his lure into the clear, fast-flowing riffle. He expertly retrieves it with a deliberate slow action to provoke the predator fish to strike.

It is a "bluebird" day in October, complete with deep blue sky, warm breeze and plenty of autumn leaves exposing their true colors now that the chlorophyll is gone.

Another cast and slow retrieve, and yet another, and then WHAM! The flexible spinning rod bends to an inverted U as the sleek game fish takes the lure into its mouth, only to find out too late that it has become the prey instead of the predator.

True to its programmed instincts, the hooked cold-blooded animal breaks for freedom by swimming hard for the nearest cover. But the six-pound test line resists the initial charge of the spirited fish as the fisherman gives it all the line necessary.

The fish tries to shake the artificial bait. In a curving slash of incredible speed it makes the water's surface boil, and then, exhausted, it's finally hauled upon the stream bank by the angler and added to the stringer.

"Where is this?" you ask. "Northern Wisconsin, or Land Between the Lakes in Kentucky?" "No," I reply. "The Great Miami River below the Third Street Bridge in downtown Dayton."

The fisherman was Leroy Curry of Parkside Homes, and the fish was a 13-inch smallmouth bass. Curry, a sophomore at Colonel White High School, and his fishing partner, Joe McNeal, caught 12 nice smallmouth bass, using "Twister Tail" lures that balmy Saturday afternoon. Two days before they had hauled out 33 of these prime game fish from the same spot.

"If you want largemouth (bass), go down to DP&L (Tait Station) and fish below the dam. You can get walleye, crappie and even catch an occasional trout there," McNeal said.

Paul Cook of West Carrollton fishes the riffles below the Third Street Bridge almost every day. "I work second trick at the Howard Paper Company, so when I get off work all I have to do is slip down the bank to the river and start fishing," Cook said. He has landed smallmouths up to 16 inches in this same spot.

Smallmouth and largemouth bass belong to the sunfish family. They are exclusively North American freshwater fish, and they feed on crayfish, small fish and minnows and insects. The smallmouth usually inhabits clear-flowing streams and large clear lakes, and are not usually found in sluggish water. On the other hand, the largemouth does well in warm, often muddy, water.

Bass spawn in the spring, using shallow "nests" excavated by the male. Much of the Miami River bottom in the downtown area is gravelly, thus providing a good habitat for these fish. In addition to making the nest, the males guard the eggs and the larval stage of the young fish.

Let's give our downtown river credit. The presence of smallmouth bass indicates a vast improvement in water quality over a few years ago. ▪

Ground Hogs Fattening Up for Their Long Winter Sleep

NOVEMBER 7, 1990

It was like Ground Hog Day in late October, except the ground hogs (woodchucks or whistle pigs) were out stuffing themselves, knowing that winter is coming. They are not much interested in the long shadow they cast in the late autumn sun.

We counted a total of eight ground hogs while riding the river bikeway on a perfect evening for such a venture. The riverbanks and levees are ideal habitat for these large hibernating animals. It offers a good place to den and plenty of food in the grasses and legumes that grow there.

These animals are dignified and deliberate, but not that powerful. They can't run very fast, and probably are not the smartest of animals, but they know enough to stay alive. That counts.

The woodchuck (ground hog) spends about ¾ of its life asleep. At this latitude their winter slumber is long and deep.

Starting about now they will hibernate in their cozy dens until late February. They pick a chamber in their underground maze, often lining it with grass, and curl up in a ball to snooze for four or five months.

This may sound like a good way to avoid creditors, paying income tax and holding the grocery budget down, but with woodchucks it is just a way of life. During their long sleep their breathing slows to just a trickle of air entering their lungs, then out. The pulse is slowed, and the animal's temperature is lowered to about 57 degrees.

Even if brought into a warm environment, it would take several hours to awake a hibernating "chuck."

So the eight woodchucks we saw the other evening were out putting on their last few ounces of "hog fat." Four of them were feeding near Deeds Point, one by Steele Dam, and there were others by the Riverbend area.

On the flagpole by the tennis courts in front of the Dayton Art Institute, a young red-tailed hawk was perched, checking out the riverbanks and floodplain for small mammals. I saw it while driving to Sinclair Community College to unload our bikes.

We left the car at Sinclair, rode up Fifth Street to just south of the Fifth Street Bridge. The steps leading down to the bikeway are slotted so that a bike can be walked down from street level.

We decided to ride the eight-mile loop counter-clockwise.

As we rode past the now-closed Central YMCA, I heard crows raising a ruckus across the river.

A look through my trusty binocs showed several crows harassing a young red-tailed hawk on a large sycamore tree along the river walkway on the McPhersontown side.

I'm sure it was the same juvenile redtail I had seen earlier, as it was only a city block upstream from the tennis courts.

The waxing moon was a little more than half full. The sun, migrating to a low southern angle, added hues to the cityscape and its slowly coloring vegetation provided warmth.

We saw two kestrels, making me wonder if one of them could possibly be "Hawkie," the female we rehabilitated a few years ago and released at Sunrise Park.

"Hawkie" was a female with a band on her left leg, but I was not able to get a good fix on the bird to check. I'm sure she is out there somewhere. ▪

Nice or Not, House Mice Certainly Are Numerous

NOVEMBER 14, 1984

I think mice
are rather nice.
Their tails are long,
their faces small,
they haven't any
chins at all.
Their ears are pink;
their teeth are white.
They run about
the house at night.
They nibble things
they shouldn't touch,
and no one seems
to like them much.
But I think mice
are nice.

—ROSE FYLEMAN

Stella, one of our five cats, moved with alert agitation from one side of the microwave cart to the other.

Something was under there, and with so many cats you would never suspect a mouse. But there it was. A small, gray-brown mouse with a naked long tail. It was about 6 ½ inches overall.

A deft thrust of the paw under the cart cause the confused mouse to emerge from cover. Here Stella's strategy broke down;

she had no idea what to do with the small intruder.

Enter Chatan, our sleek, jet-black, streetwise outdoor cat—a killer of birds, including pigeons. One pounce, and it was all over. Chatan and his prey were promptly ushered outside, and the case was closed.

The house mouse, Mus musculus, is a native of Asia, where it colonized the Mediterranean region even before Rome was its center. They came to America about the time of the Revolution and have accompanied humans into every state.

According to Victor H. Cahalane, a scholarly zoologist and editor of *The Imperial Collection of Audubon Animals*, states in his text on the house mouse, "Rats outnumber humans, and there are twice as many house mice as rats."

George Freck, my Future Farmers of America teacher in high school, always said a good rule of thumb was, "If you see one mouse, you have at least ten."

In our area, mice seek shelter in buildings this time of year. In three years of living downtown, I have seen only this one mouse in our house.

House mice are sociable animals and they colonize. Each mouse family is dominated by one male, who has one or more females. The happy family has a nest of paper, rags and other trash, sometimes including grass. They come out at night, and if they find plenty of food they might travel only a few yards from their nest site.

They can climb, jump and swim, and when thoroughly alarmed, they can run at the fast clip of 12 feet per second. They breed from early spring to late fall and can raise five to ten litters each year with five-eight babies per litter. They are born in 19 days naked and blind, weighing about ½ ounce. They develop fast, and in three weeks they are weaned. At six weeks they're capable of bearing young.

Thank goodness for cats.

One pair of mice has tremendous breeding potential in just one year. To calculate this, you must assume eight litters per year per breeding pair and eight mice in each litter. Remember, too, that every six weeks each pair of house mice will reproduce again, and the newborn mice will breed at six weeks of age and every six weeks thereafter. The average house mouse lives about a year.

So take a bow, Chatan, Stella, Rafer, Tux, and Henry, for keeping that mouse population down. ▪

Bikeway Perfect for a November Bike-Hike

The best eight miles in Dayton is the River Corridor Bikeway, round trip, between Island Park and the Stewart Street Bridge.

For bikers, joggers or hikers, it's a great place to be on a mid-November day when the sky is clear blue and temperatures are in the sixties. If you're a naturalist, it's even better. The diversity along the bikeway is exciting and ever changing.

The river helps. After nearly 200 years of intense civilization there is still an abundance of natural history along the banks of the Great Miami River and its downtown tributaries. Get your binoculars and a notebook, and let's take an eight-mile nature bike-hike.

The wind is powerful enough to spin the Dayton Power and Light wind generator at Sinclair Community College, which means a velocity of at least ten but with gusts up to 30 miles per hour.

I recommend riding downstream on the west side of the river and let the high bank be your windbreak. Then, while riding upstream, you will have a tail wind. Let's enter the bikeway at River's Edge, just behind the YMCA, and travel upstream.

Beyond the Main Street Bridge a patch of green will catch your eye. Plants are growing out of the cracks of a massive limestone retainer wall, Kenilworth ivy full of tiny blooms, probably planted there or escaped from some downtown flower garden years ago. The flower is mauve, with a white and yellow lip. It blooms from

May to October. But here it is, the second week of November and we've had severe frosts and temperatures in the low 20s.

A gravel bar in the Mad River below the new Dayton Board of Education Career Academy sports more blooms. Perhaps the river affects some temperature control on cold nights, or maybe the plants are just winter hardy. But here are bur marigold, white aster, river purslane and boneset, all in bloom.

We spot five pied-billed grebes, small chicken-like water birds, diving in the lagoon at Island Park.

After crossing the river at Helena Street Bridge, it is windy for a short distance, until we drop over the bank behind Riverbend Art Center.

Here among a flock of 12 resident mallard ducks is a pair of common pintails, cousins to the mallard. The male has a white breast, slim neck, and a long, needle pointed tail. A conspicuous white point runs from the neck up onto the side of its head. The female is similar in appearance to the female mallard.

At the mouth of the Mad River a male gadwall duck, another migratory relative of the mallard, is seen with a raft of about 30 mallards. The gadwall is not as easy to identify as the beautifully marked pintail. Seldom diving, these puddle ducks feed by dabbling in shallow waters with bills down and tails up.

Wolf Creek is crystal clear, and if the beer cans and tires and floating mattress were not there it would look like a pristine stream. We can easily see a large school of small fish through the clear water, but they are hard to identify. A shadow sends a thousand three- to four-inch fish in all directions.

Traveling past St. Elizabeth Hospital and up the bank we encounter the full blast of stiff wind. As we cross the Stewart Street Bridge, a good tail wind carries us swiftly northward up the bikeway. Mallards, pigeons, red clover in bloom and robins feeding on Washington hawthorn berries are all worth noting.

Between the Salem Avenue Bridge and the low dam, we spot a big grey bird standing about two feet tall. It looks much like an oversized pigeon. My binoculars bring the bird eight times closer. It's an immature herring gull, commonly called a seagull, stopping by Dayton to feed in the Great Miami. They spend the summer from Lake Erie north to northern Canada, then push southward to the warm sunny beaches of the Gulf States and to Florida. I know that this is a young bird, two or three years old, as their adult plumage does not show until the third of fourth spring after hatching.

Would you believe, violets and dandelions in bloom, and up on the flood control levee some Siberian elms have green leaves? Some plants just don't realize it's nearly winter! ▪

Squirrels Find Their Hidden Cache; Do They Sniff it out, or is it Memory?

NOVEMBER 29, 1989

We have wild critters living downtown whose economic prowess would give Citizen's Federal or any well-managed thrift a "run for the money."

Historically, these critters were here long before we came into the picture. The sat in the trees and chattered as Indians hunted in the wide valley where three rivers converged. They watched as the Native Americans retreated to higher ground because of the floodwaters. They scolded as the first boatload of European settlers landed in the big bend of the river and began to build their cabins on the flat, wide valley in spite of floods.

If gray squirrels could record history, I'm sure their commentary on our species would be cutting. Our struggle to improve our lot, maintain dignity, and, yes, finally dedicate some serious commitment to how we manage the air, water, and land that makes up our environment would be critically assessed if squirrels could study and comment on us.

But, squirrels have a mental capacity limited to simple stimulus response behavior, and it is we who are able to record history. Comments on squirrel economy are based upon our studies of them and interpreting the results of research in terms of human values.

All of this is a long introduction to the fact that squirrels have a good economy in spite of their lack of brains. During three months of the year, they deposit heavily into their savings accounts and for nine months survive by withdrawing from these "funds." The system seems to work for them. It consists simply of burying more nuts than are needed for the long, hard winter.

Dr. Lucia Jacobs completed her doctoral dissertation attempting to determine if squirrels can remember where they bury their nuts or if they randomly dig up their cache by smell. Her excellent article in the October 1989 issue of *Natural History* magazine, entitled "Cache Economy of the Gray Squirrel," reveals some fascinating behavior of the bushy-tailed rodent.

While on the campus of Princeton University, Jacobs cared for many an orphaned baby gray squirrel in her dormitory room, feeding them on soft foods and milk until adolescence.

Without benefit of parental training and role modeling, the young squirrels, after weeks of soft dormitory life, behaved almost robotically when presented with their first nut.

"The squirrels performed flawlessly from the first day," Jacobs wrote in her article. "I was fascinated as I observed these miniature squirrels pick up a hazelnut for the first time, search intently for a suitable burying site, and then, with great zest, dig a hole with both paws flying, the nut firmly clenched between tiny teeth, with all the confidence and success of a jaded park squirrel burying its millionth nut."

These pampered orphans behaved as other gray squirrels have behaved for thousands of years, by burying each nut in a separate hole.

Jacobs' challenge was, "Do they remember where they store their nuts?"

The gray squirrel has life-and-death dependency on stored food. Rather than store a cache of nuts or acorns in a nice dry hollow tree, it chooses to store one nut per hole in the ground. If not eaten during the winter the "planted" nut will sprout and grow.

Jacobs called this scattered hoarding, purposeful behavior that enables the "owner" of the nut some degree of assurance that no one else can find it.

For years, biologists accepted the claim of mammalogist Victor H. Cahalane, *Mammals of North America*, (MacMillan Company, 1947) who stated, "It appears that squirrels use their memory to reach the vicinity of their caches, after which they rely on their sensitive noses." Jacobs' research showed that gray squirrels rely a great deal more on memory than had previously been believed.

"Even a few weeks of heavy snow each winter may produce a sufficient selective pressure to maintain a gray squirrel's memory," she concluded.

I know one thing for sure, with my memory, I would have a tough time making it through the winter. ▪

Raccoon's Circles Under Eyes from Sleepless Nights?

NOVEMBER 29, 1991

"Don't shoot, colonel, I'll come down. I know I'm a gone coon."

The excerpt from a story by David Crockett (1786-1836) about a treed raccoon aptly describes the plight of a downtown raccoon found huddled in a window well at the city building recently by Goodie Gillespie, business manager for the city's division of property management.

Gillespie and some associates at the time were putting the Christmas decorations on City Hall.

"The poor raccoon had apparently fallen or jumped into the deep window well and was unable to get out," Gillespie said. "When I found it, it was sort of crouched and shivering in a corner of the well, and at first I wasn't sure what to do."

If raccoon thoughts could be expressed, I'm sure Crockett's expression would fit. (You remember Davy Crockett, king of the wild frontier?)

Incidentally, the term "gone coon" originated during the Revolutionary War days as a plea from a spy dressed in raccoon skins who had just been discovered by an English rifleman.

Most people easily recognize raccoons. They have brown-ish-grey fur, roundish bodies, a ringed tail and a black Lone Ranger-type mask covering their eyes. Behind the mask, dark brown eyes peer intently at you. This causes humans to use such description as "cute, cuddly, curious, comical and lovable."

Having a lot of experience with raccoons, I would add "mischievous, tough, cantankerous, bold, tenacious and tough" to the list, with a word of caution to anyone who might want to pet a wild raccoon.

They are not uncommon to downtown Dayton. They have adapted to most urban environments by living in underground storm water systems and other tunnel networks, which are readily available and are suitable homes for animals that originally lived in hollow trees. Food is not a problem, since ample scraps of choice morsels are scattered about. There are plenty of garbage cans and garden plots for easy picking.

Jack Gottschang, a retired zoologist from the University of Cincinnati, has studied urban raccoons in that city and found that their population often exceeds that of rural woodlands.

Gillespie said that after finding the animal, which he described as fully-grown, he treated it as if it were his own.

"I'm used to seeing coons around my house on Otterbein Avenue. I really like seeing them, as well as the birds that come to our seven bird feeders. I love watching animals, and caring for them. It is a real source of peace to me."

He called several places before locating a naturalist at the Dayton-Montgomery County Park District, who removed the raccoon with a harness, caged it and then released it safely in a public wooded area.

The scientific name for raccoon is *Procyon lotor*. The first part, *Procyon*, is a Greek word meaning "before the dog." It has to do with the brightest star in the constellation Canis Minor, which rises before the dog star, Sirius.

Why this name was given to the raccoon, I am not sure—unless it has something to do with coon hunting. Lotor literally means, "a washer" and refers to the raccoon habit of supposedly washing its food before eating it. Some biologists say this is not so, that the animal is just dabbling the food before eating it, which stimulates their search along streams for aquatic prey.

We feed raccoons at home using generic dog food. A dish of water is provided at the feeding station along with the dog food. Using both front paws, the raccoons lift a handful of food out of the bowl, place it in the water and then proceed to eat the messy, mushy, dissolved dog food.

Raccoons are nocturnal, and the best time to observe them is on a warm, rainy night during the winter months. They do not hibernate, but stay in their dens during the extremely cold or snowy weather. They usually have one litter per year, averaging four young. Most litters are born in April or May, but I have seen young raccoons at our feeding station in October.

For a long time hunters have sought raccoons for fur and meat. Raccoon hunting is a night sport, usually done with dog and gun, with the highest success on warm, rainy nights following a thaw. ▪

Loud, Smart Bird Spends This Time of Year Flocking, Feeding

DECEMBER 7, 1988

*("Tis) the many wintered crow that
leads the clanging rookery home.*

TENNYSON

This is the time of the year that crows are usually in large, raucous flocks ranging widely in search of food. Downtown crows probably fare better than their rural counterparts in that they only have to range to the nearest garbage can that may have been ransacked the night before by a fat, happy storm-sewer-dwelling raccoon.

Or they may spend their time profitably hunting morsels along the Great Miami River. Frequently they perch in the large dead tree along Roberts Drive between Salem Avenue and the Third Street Bridge, and scour the river's edge for tidbits.

Crows, familiar to everyone, are members of the Corvidae family of birds, as are jays, ravens and magpies. They are always described as bold, inquisitive, and highly adaptable with loud, harsh voices. In addition, they eat almost anything.

What more could you want from a bird that is programmed for survival?

Often, during late autumn and early spring, crows will congregate in large, communal roosts. The last one of these I recall was in Miamisburg a few years ago. The flock numbered in the thousands. Another was spotted near Clark State Community College, near Springfield, last year.

Unfortunately, crow roosts are not as common as they were 25 to 30 years ago. This may be due to the loss of habitat and possibly sport hunting. So little research has been done on the common crow that their population dynamics are not easily understood.

If you hear or happen to see a roost, let us know and we will notify readers of the exact location.

As a social pastime, crows enjoy mobbing birds of prey. Three years ago in a *Downtowner* column, I covered the fascinating visit of a great horned owl to the downtown neighborhood.

This was not altogether planned on the part of the owl. I later learned that the owl, an apparent resident of Woodlawn Cemetery near the University of Dayton, had been forced to leave home at the behest of a flock of angry crows.

I received the tip from an 80-year old woman who lives at the Moraine Apartments, 27 S. Ludlow Street. She called and excitedly related that something was going on across Ludlow Street near Arcade Square and that it had something to do with crows. She could not see the owl, but later I called her and explained the whole story.

A nice thing about crows is that they are smart. In fact, I believe crows are the smartest birds in the world. David Quammen, in his book, *Natural Acts, A Sidelong View of Science and Nature*, writes "And, probably, according to my theory, they are too bright for their own good. You know the pattern. Time on their hands. Under-employed and over qualified. Large amounts of potential just lying fallow. Pick up a little corn, knock back a few grasshoppers, carry a beak full of dead rabbit home for the kids, then fly over to sit on a fence rail with eight or ten cronies and watch some poor farmer sweat like a sow at the wheel of his tractor. An easy enough life, but is this it? Is this all?" ▪

Once Plentiful, Black Bears Have Disappeared

DECEMBER 16, 1992

Deer, woodchucks, raccoon and 'possum have been seen downtown, but so far no black bears.

But just wait.

"Black bears were once common in Ohio," says Jim Petrasek, Ohio Division of Wildlife, law enforcement supervisor in northeast Ohio.

"It is believed that the last native bear was killed in Paulding County (northwest of Lima) in 1881. In the early 1970s, biologists from the Division's Akron office were hearing reports of bear sightings in counties bordering Pennsylvania," says Petrasek.

"This summer, residents of Ashtabula County reported a black bear scavenging in garbage bags full of graduation leftovers. After roaming northern Ashtabula County for a week, the bear had firmly established itself as a nuisance.

"Since the bear had little fear of humans, wildlife officers trapped it, put an identification tag on it and transported it to the remote wooded areas of southern Ohio. It was hoped that the bear would adapt to its natural surroundings and avoid additional associations with humans. Six days later the bear was shot in Kentucky, where it had continued to call attention to its presence by raiding the dumpster at a riverside restaurant."

We probably won't see black bears in Dayton, but a few years ago, few downtowners would have believed that deer would be swimming downstream of the Main Street Bridge—you never know about these wild critters. ▪

How Homer Gave Up Catching Birds for Watching PBS

It was a year ago on Friday, December 13, 1985, that we captured Homer at Leland Center on Siebenthaler Avenue and brought him to our downtown condo.

Homer is a young, black, domesticated cat that had spent several days at the Dayton-Montgomery County Park District headquarters catching juncos and eating them. He showed no signs of being owned, and exhibited all the signs of stealth and patience necessary to catch apparently healthy birds for his daily sustenance.

The initial ride to our house on Riverview Terrace was traumatic for Homer. He had to be pried from a safe cranny under the seat of my station wagon. Once in the house he streaked for the safety under the first upholstered chair available at his new address.

Tux, Stella and Henry, our other cats, were busy asserting their territorial imperative, stimulated by this stranger in their midst. Daunted by the growling and spitting of three peers, Homer sought refuge in the basement, there to remain for the better part of the next two months.

Finally, with consistent coaxing, he slowly began to trust us. He started coming upstairs for food and water, while at the same time gaining some acceptance from the three other cats that live here.

He was living in a fool's paradise, daring to trust human beings who believe that the only good cat is a de-sexed, de-clawed cat. After his operation, Homer has been transformed into a totally dependent but very lovable household pet.

For his anniversary gift, we invited Homer and his three peers to watch *Nature*, the Public Broadcasting System Sunday night show entitled *Cats*. George Page, and his cat, Clyde were the narrators.

Page explained that cats have been associating with people for more than 4,000 years. They are now America's number one pet. He described them as independent, aloof, mysterious, and the most perfectly designed predators on the planet.

By this time Tux, who is 17, was ZZZZ'ed out on the couch. Henry, who possesses a low tolerance for strange sounds, split the moment the television was turned on. Homer and Stella sat in their usual feline posture facing the opposite direction from the tube. We ignored them and continued to enjoy the program.

Homer and Stella were not impressed.

But suddenly the shrill scream of cats mating and engaging in confrontation caused our cats to respond with enthusiasm and some anxiety. Cat ears are considerably more sensitive than ours. These sounds drew Homer to within inches of the tube.

Standing, with his clawless paws resting on the rim of the picture tube, he viewed the show for some three minutes from this position. Tux, awakened by the squawk of mating female cats, soon went back to sleep. Stella, attracted by the same sound, jumped up on the couch and watched the show from some eight feet away.

Homer backed away slowly, maintaining his gaze from electronically transmitted cats and mice and sat down on the floor where he continued to watch alertly for another six to eight minutes. ▪

Annual Christmas Bird Count Yields a Few Surprises

DECEMBER 25, 1991

On Sunday, December 15, the 67th annual Audubon Christmas Bird Count, sponsored by the Dayton Audubon Society, brought out 40 avid birders to count our wintering and resident bird populations.

In 1900, ornithologist Frank Chapman, then editor of *Bird Lore*, asked Audubon Society members to devote part of Christmas Day to counting birds. In response, 27 people in 26 localities took part. Ben Blincoe led the first Dayton-area winter census in 1925.

In Dayton, twelve groups set out early Sunday morning in weather that included snow squalls and temperatures ranging from a high of 30 to a low of 10 degrees.

The downtown group that I usually led was under the guidance of David Dister, a biologist with Woolpert Consultants. Priscilla and I were doing the Christmas Bird Count in Corpus Christi, Texas, where the Sunday morning weather was more agreeable. Although a cold front brought the low down to 48 degrees, chilly for the south Texas coast, the high was near 60 degrees.

The downtown Dayton group covered parks and the river corridor from the railroad bridge below Fifth Street, upstream to the old Frigidaire Park on the Stillwater River, and up the Great Miami River to Kittyhawk Golf Course. This diverse habitat of rivers, woods and meadows produced a real variety of birds, in spite of the cold. Two eastern screech owls at Wegerzyn Horticultural Center and eight green-winged teal ducks on a small puddle at Kittyhawk were the only reports of these species from the twelve groups.

A northern flicker (woodpecker) was spotted exhibiting unusual behavior by flying into a snow squall near old Frigidaire Park.

The group found several species considered rare for winter. A winter wren at Wegerzyn, the green-winged teal, a sharp-shinned hawk and six killdeer, which they found in the north pond of Wegerzyn, are still listed in the official Dayton Audubon Society bird checklist as rare in winter.

"Probably the rarest sighting for the downtown group," Dister said, "was across the Stillwater River from old Frigidaire Park, where we saw what appeared to be a large green parrot. Checking the *Peterson Field Guide*, we decided it must be a black-hooded parakeet, a South American resident, and certainly an escape from someone's house. It was amazing! This tropical bird was apparently surviving the cold."

In Texas, our Christmas Bird Count included green-winged teal, 75 of them wintering in Oso Bay in the Hans Suter Wildlife Park in Corpus Christi. Oso Bay contains a sizeable saltwater marsh and open-water area and is part of the Corpus Christi Bay system. High counts of green-winged teal were recorded in 1987 at Cypress Creek, Texas, near Houston, where 12,350 green-wings were counted.

It is a pleasure to see these small, colorful puddle ducks. In fact, this is the smallest of the dabbling ducks, about half the size of the familiar mallard. They have a grey body with a brown head that shows a broad greenish eye patch in the sunlight. In flight, they flash a deep, iridescent green on the upper sides of the wings. They are fast, agile, and fly in a characteristic tight formation.

Out Texas count included many birds we were seeing for the first time, such as kiskadees, green kingfishers, green jays, gold-fronted woodpeckers, crested caracaras, and black-bellied whistling ducks.

Our most exciting first, which we want to share with you later in more detail, occurred at Aransas National Wildlife Refuge, about 70 miles north of Corpus Christi. We were fortunate to see an adult pair of North America's tallest birds, the rare/endangered whooping crane. Only 200 of these birds exist in the world and 133 of them have returned to winter in Aransas. They stand about 5 ½ feet tall, with a wingspan of more than seven feet.

Jim Hill, compiler for Dayton, said several records were set this year. "We had a record number of blue jays, 115," he said. Many of them were seen at Aullwood Farm near Englewood.

"We counted 27 eastern bluebirds, 25 Bonaparte's gulls and 48 red-bellied woodpeckers that made new records for the 67-year history," said Hill.

In Dayton the total count for the day was 61 different species. In the Corpus Christi area, counts ran from 147 to 198 species. ■

Plants Figure Out the Best Time to Bloom

JANUARY 9, 1985

Forsythia is blooming in Sunrise Park. Bush honeysuckle is in flower behind the Central YMCA, 117 W. Monument Avenue. Dandelions are blooming in other downtown locations, including the river floodplain.

Plants are able to respond to a wide variety of environmental situations because they have systems for monitoring important environmental factors, such as light and temperature.

Plants grow individually as coordinated units, with one part having a big influence on the growth and development of another part. This influence may be through food, light source, water supply, or the production and distribution of hormones.

Hormones are natural compounds produced within the plant and transported to the site of action within the plant, in this case, the flower buds. This chemical system consists of things called auxins, gibberellins, cytokinins, abscisic acid and ethylene, all working in harmony to bring about plant growth.

You normally expect to see forsythia, bush honeysuckle and dandelions bloom around the time of the vernal (spring) equinox (March 21).

Forsythia is a native shrub of Europe and Asia and a member of the Olive family. It is planted here mostly as a hedge or ornamental cluster to hail the coming of spring. I'll use it as an example of a plant whose internal regulators permit flowers to appear in the early spring before its leaves. So why is it blooming in December and early January?

An easy explanation is the record warm weather we experienced, but there's more to it than that.

First, you must consider the big picture as it relates to plant blooming. Its purpose is not to provide beauty for human beings, but to perpetuate the species through seed reproduction.

Let's explore the regulating mechanism that allows a plant to tell time so that flower and seed production will occur at the most favorable periods. It involves a substance called phytochrome, which responds to day (or night) lengths and is able to measure differences as small as 10 minutes in a photoperiod (day length).

There are long-day plants, such as the bluegrass in your lawn, which will bloom increasingly well (when unmowed) during days that are 12-14 hours in length. Then there are short-day plants, chrysanthemums, for example. These plants will bloom early in the spring or late in autumn as controlled by their light-sensitive regulators.

Other plants fall into the category of day neutral, meaning they require no particular day length. The day neutral species may respond to temperature, water stress (too much or too little) or they may be genetically programmed to bloom regardless of environmental conditions.

Forsythia falls in the day neutral category. It's blooming because of the warm weather and not the length of the day. The flower buds in this case have been exposed to enough warm weather to "break dormancy" and signal to the plant that it is safe to make flowers.

Keep an eye on forsythia to see if it is blooming now and also to note what happens when its regular flowering period comes around in the spring.

Through the phenomenon of photoperiodism, most plants do bloom precisely with the seasons. Day length also affects the egg-laying behavior of mites, snails, bass and morning doves. And it determines the migration direction of birds and the mating times of horses and sheep. ▪

McPherson Town Trees Not a Bore for Columnist

JANUARY 13, 1993

McPherson Town is well known for its giant hackberry trees.

This historic section of town just north of the Great Miami River levee has, I would guess, the largest hackberry trees in Dayton. In fact, on the levee, contrary to the Miami Conservancy District's policy of no trees, some very large hackberry and sycamore trees are growing.

I asked Jim Rozelle, general manage and chief engineer of the district, why the exceptions to the rule.

"These trees were grandfathered in," Rozelle answered. "I don't know how old they are, but everyone believes they were there before the present levee, and probably before the 1913 flood."

He added, "Trees can be a serious detriment to flood control during a peak flooding period—they can wash out, catch debris, and ultimately cause levee failure."

I asked him if he had any problem with my attempting to determine the age of a few of these trees. He had none.

Trees may be aged in two ways:

1. Cut the tree down and count the annual growth rings from the outside of the stump to the center. This method is 100% accurate, but it tends to be hard on the tree.

2. Measure the tree with a forester's diameter tape to determine its diameter in inches, and then drill into the tree with another tool used by foresters called an increment

borer. This is a long drill bit with threads that "screw" into the tree.

The borer bit has a hollow center, enabling one to extract a core or cross-section from the trunk of the tree. With this core in hand you can count the growth rings per inch of the cross section, then multiply the rings times tree radius and you have the age of the tree. And the tree is still alive.

There are even tiny pills that can be slipped into the hole left in the tree to prevent diseases from entering.

I applied this process to the large sycamore tree just west of the Main Street Bridge on the river's side of the levee and to an even larger hackberry tree downstream near Floral Drive across from Ed Smith's Flowers.

I had two assistants, young residents of McPherson Town just home from school. Kalin Lewis McDonald and Jeremy Lee Cox seemed very interested in what I was doing and I was pleased to explain the whole thing to them.

As we twisted the increment borer into the big sycamore to extract the core, the boys were most interested in helping by turning the sturdy handle. We pulled out a core, counted the annual growth rings, and came up with an average of 10 rings per inch.

"I figure this sycamore is about 130 to 150 years old." I told the boys, "but to be more accurate, let's take a boring on the other side of the tree."

The other side was facing the river and the steep levee caused us to have to descend a foot or two lower to drill the hole on the south side of the tree. As the increment borer reached its maximum depth in the tree, I put the extractor in to take out the core and nothing came out. A moment later, water squirted out—right out of the end of the hollow borer still inserted in the tree—just as if we had turned on a water faucet.

Jeremy said, "That's sap—that's the stuff birds eat. You can make syrup out of that."

I explained that we had apparently tapped into a hollow "reservoir" in the center of the tree.

The error factor of increment borer aging can be as high as plus or minus five percent—so I think some history is established here. This, of course, means that the tree survived the 1913 flood.

Could it be that the gap in large trees along the present levee west of the Main Street Bridge could be accounted for by assuming that this is where the levee failed 80 years ago this March, and some sycamores were washed away?

I aged a large hackberry on the river side of the levee, at Floral Drive and Riverview. It is 32.2 inches in diameter, but only 105 years old, just a mere sapling in 1913. It appears that the present levee was constructed with these trees in place.

If anyone has more information on the history of the levee trees west of the Main Street Bridge, I would appreciate a call at 898-3495. ▪

Going to Bat for Walley: Rescued Bat Almost Done with Rehab, Doing Well

FEBRUARY 3, 1993

Happy day after Groundhog Day—winter is still with us.

Walley, the bat rescued from the side of Gem Savings Building at Third and Main Streets, is alive and healthy at Brukner Nature Center in Miami County.

Vicki Keever, receptionist for CityWide Development, had discovered Walley clinging to the side of the Gem City Savings Building on the second floor.

She was concerned that the bat might suffer from the cold, having seen it in the same spot for two days. She and co-workers Bob Murray and Rhonda McDonald convinced Don Johnson, an employee of Ace Window Cleaning, to put his ladders up to the bat's perch and make the rescue.

Safely tucked into a box, they delivered the bat to John Ritzenthaler, a naturalist at the Aullwood Audubon Center in Butler Township.

Ritzenthaler identified it as Little Brown Bat, and since Aullwood has no facility for rehabilitating animals, Walley was transported to Brukner Nature Center. At Brukner, located near the Scenic Stillwater River in Miami County, animal rehab is part of their program.

I called Joan Heidelberg, co-director with husband Bob, of Brukner Nature Center. She told me that Walley was receiving a diet of mealworms, was gaining weight, and would soon be released.

The story may continue at that point, since bats have a strong homing instinct and Walley may yearn for the hustle and bustle of downtown and make the return trip of about 20 miles.

A final note on Walley—Keever told me that after the Dayton Daily News article, they received a number of phone calls complimenting them on rescuing the little bat and that Ace Window Cleaning's phone had been "ringing off the hook" thanking them for their "brave deed." ▪

House Finch Adds Song and Color to City

FEBRUARY 17, 1988

I introduced downtowners to the house finch a few years ago after discovering a nesting pair in Jane Reece Park at Salem and Riverview Avenues. They look and act a lot like house sparrows and adapt well to the urban environment.

If purple finches can be described as sparrows dipped in raspberry juice, then the house finch must have been dipped in tomato juice. In the drab central city winter, the house finch adds color and song. In the case of the Carpodacus mexicanus (house finch) the bright red male and striped brown female may be heard nearly everywhere downtown where trees are big enough to provide a stage for singing. The voice is very finch-like, bright and airy, but loose and disjointed. Notes of the male house finch sometimes sound like the common house sparrow, but more musical.

It has been more than 50 years now since a shipment of illegal house finches came from California to New York City for sale in the birdcage trade. With federal agents in hot pursuit, some pet store owners let the birds fly the coop out the back door as the lawmen entered the front.

The result was the establishment of an eastern population of this opportunistic bird, known before only west of the Rockies. *Birds of America*, a voluminous publication of 1971, describes the distribution of the house finch at that time as "western United States and northern Mexico, east to the western border of the Great Plains."

These finches do not appear to migrate. Their songs may be heard even now in the large trees along the Miami River at Van Cleve Park, in the Oregon Historic District and at Sinclair Community College.

I spotted a singing male in the linden trees just west of the construction of Building 12 recently. As I approached, the bird flushed and flew to the underside of the walkway between buildings two and ten, two stories up. Here the bird disappeared above the light fixture, a choice that would provide a warm roost during sub-zero nights, and an excellent nesting site.

Finches also belong to a large family of birds called the Fringillidae. They have cone-shaped bills, eat mostly weeds and seeds and are less migratory than many birds.

Other common downtown birds that are members of the finch family include the beautiful red cardinal, the white throated sparrow, the goldfinch, the junco and the song sparrow.

The house finch belongs to a different family, the weaver finch, Ploceidae. Although they, too, have large bills adapted for seed eating, their diet trends toward insects.

Older writings often attempted to justify birds by citing their economic value as weed seed and insect consumers. *Birds of America* discussed the value of finches. Assuming their combined consumption of weed seed was enough to save one percent of the nine billion dollar agricultural crop of 1910, this family of birds would have been worth nine million dollars to the United States economy.

Throughout its range the house finch has made itself feel at home where we do. As the name implies, it likes to be around human habitation, but it seems less of a pest than the house sparrow.

My observations have been that it seems more tree-oriented and less apt to clutter your eaves and various openings around your house with nesting material. ▪

High-flying Downtown Residents Here to Stay

FEBRUARY 24, 1993

It looks like two of downtown Dayton's most prominent residents are here to stay. No, they don't have names like Huffman or Patterson, but rather Falco peregrinus—peregrine falcons or rather less formally, Rachel and Mercury.

If you aren't up to speed on their story, here's a brief summary of last year's falcon activity. They arrived in Dayton last year, possibly as early as September 1991, and took up housekeeping on the old Lazarus Building at Second and Ludlow Streets.

They immediately attracted a cadre of downtown falcon watchers, and the Ohio Division of Wildlife office in Xenia formally organized the Falcon Patrol, a group of down-towners who keep careful records of the birds' whereabouts and activities.

They established a nest in a window box on the west side of the Second and Ludlow Street corner. They were easy to see from the top stories of the parking garage on the other side of Ludlow. For a while they seemed to be serious about building a nest and laying eggs. But nothing happened.

Rachel, it turned out, was a subadult, too young to lay fertile eggs. So the two birds gradually gave up the idea of nesting and rearing young and began to fly farther from downtown to hunt the only thing they eat—other birds, which they catch by diving upon them in flight.

Peregrine falcons are the fastest birds in the world and those lucky enough to see one of them make a strike in midair never forget it.

Some observers reported seeing them as far south as the University of Dayton. Still, they usually returned to the Lazarus Building to roost for the night.

Their daytime flights made it more and more difficult to see them around what had become their daytime haunts when they were still trying to nest.

There is a good chance of nesting success this year. Stan Staggs, a downtowner and member of the Falcon Patrol, reports the addition of two new nesting boxes on the west and south sides of the Lazarus Building.

Spring 1993 holds more promise because both birds should become nearly capable of a successful hatch of young peregrines.

If this happens, we will be fortunate, indeed. Peregrines have been introduced in most of the major cities in Ohio by now, but only Toledo has a successful hatching of young in 1992.

Peregrine falcons were virtually wiped out by pesticides, mainly DDT, in the 1960s and 1970s. Programs of captive breeding and release in the wild, both in the United States and Canada, are showing encouraging results.

DDT was banned in both countries early in the 1970s, but is still used in many Latin American countries. Birds wintering there still pick up significant quantities of pesticides.

Last summer my wife, Priscilla, and I saw peregrines in their natural nesting grounds in the cliffs beside the Mackenzie River far above the Arctic Circle near Inuvik, Northwest Territories, Canada. We heard one scream and recognized the sound immediately because we had heard it before, amazingly, in downtown Dayton. ▪

Spring Signaled by Robin's Arrival

FEBRUARY 28, 1990

The north wind doth blow,
And we shall have snow,
And what will poor robin do then?
Poor thing.
He'll sit in a barn
To keep himself warm
And hide his head under his wing.
Poor thing.

AUTHOR UNKNOWN

February is gone.

It flew by like it was shot out of a cannon.

March, the wonderfully tempestuous month of spring, welcomes us. The vernal equinox is just 20 days away—the first day of spring.

As if on schedule, the "first robin to arrive" has been spotted at Dave Hall Plaza Park and others were seen in Jane Reece Park. Out in the suburbs large flocks of robins have been sighted, and the big question is, "Did they ever leave?"

Local birders know that robins are here year-round. The Audubon Christmas Bird Counts here have produced robins over 50 times in the last 65 years, with 1,392 being spotted in December 1964. But this spring harbinger remains as traditional as skunk cabbage, the first wildflower to bloom in these parts, and excited people still call to report the first robin of spring.

The bird's ability to vary its diet helps it survive the rigors of winter months. When the snow flies robins switch from worms and insect larva to seeds and berries, which also means a shift from feeding on the ground to getting food in shrubs and trees.

Through March, expect to see your favorite robins establish a territory and get serious about nesting.

Robin nesting has been observed as early as late February, but will probably peak about mid-May.

The first sign of mating behavior begins with the break-up of the old gang of males that hung around together during the winter. Males become less tolerant of other males and actually begin attacking and displaying aggressive action toward each other.

Accompanying this aggression is the establishment of territories. Males will be confining their individual movements to about one acre, but these territories may overlap considerably with those of other males.

As soon as the females arrive, the territory shrinks to about one-third acre and protection intensifies.

Here the betrothed pair will build its nest of grass mixed with mud.

If you locate a robin territory, look for the nesting behavior and try to locate the nest. In downtown parks and green spaces, look in evergreens and sturdy shrubs as well as horizontal man-made structures.

I have often seen them nesting in stoplights and street lamps around our urban neighborhood.

The nest may be anywhere from five to 30 feet off the ground. The nest's outside diameter will be from six to eight inches. ▪

Trees Important to Future of Main Street

MARCH 7, 1990

"Main Street is our great commons. It belongs to all of us," said Paul Woodie, director of planning for the city of Dayton, at the recent City Sessions meeting, and John Gower, the city's downtown planner, discussed the Main Street Project.

Woodie continued, "It represents the culture, commerce and history of our city. The street, trees, public art, lighting, public spaces, buildings, uses and functions must work together to animate Main Street in a vision shared by the entire community. Main Street is for everyone and it is more than bricks and mortar."

At the recent meeting, more than 200 people packed Lazarus's auditorium to hear and comment on the project designed to improve the appearance of Main Street.

It is encouraging to see the high degree of interest in this project. Just two weeks ago at the Convention Center, a similar sized audience showed much enthusiasm when the National Park Service and the 2003 Committee held a public forum to discuss the creation of a National Park in Dayton dedicated to the city's role in aviation history.

Various concepts and visions have been put forth on improving Main Street since 1948, when the Civil War Monument was moved to Sunrise Park, west of the Miami River. This facilitated making Main Street a thoroughfare for downtown, Woodie said.

"The 1190 plan will provide for better traffic flow by channeling it—narrowing vehicular space and widening the area for activities and streetscape design," he said.

Gower presented the current vision for Main Street using the analogy of designing the living space within a room. The streetscape, or floor, will incorporate trees, public art and street furniture. The walls or buildings could be enhanced with "lighting of high character to celebrate great building facades, sculpted rooflines, the tracery of tree branches. It should provide a visual sense of warmth and excitement."

I listened with interest to the presentations at City Sessions and then read the handouts, *A Planning and Design Perspective* and *Downtown Opportunities Plan—Annual Update*. I was searching, mainly, for an indication of how, when, and where more trees would be planted in the new design.

A recently completed model, "The Greening of Main Street—1990" was displayed, showing a lot of trees to be planted in the new design. It is now on display at the Living City Center, Fifth and Ludlow Streets.

In the narrative on Streetscape, trees are lumped into a discussion on vertical elements along with poles and sculptures. It is recommended that their placement reflect the formal geometric patterns, design and sight lines of Main Street.

The recommendation reads: "Street trees should be placed in such a manner to enhance the view and vistas of Main Street and some of its best architecture, and not block and hide them. Species of trees should be chosen for scale and similarity and character of tree canopy habits."

Street trees are an expensive aesthetic. In the adverse environment of downtown, they have an average life of about 12 years. It takes 40 or more years to produce a tree that adds substantially to the cooling of hot summer days and the oxygen supply. Every effort should be made to locate suitable sites for planting trees that could mature and provide a canopy. Main Street trees will be subject to great stress: heat, shade, pollution, vandalism and lack of water, but rows of trees that have to be replaced every 10 years are better than no trees at all.

Looking around at the Center City's nooks, crannies and vacant lots reveals that the "Tree of Heaven" species, or Ailanthus, might be a good bet for tree planting. It is a tree that seeds naturally and grows in the worst of habitats. In Boston it is called the Ghetto Palm and in Chicago it is used extensively for small park and street plantings.

Another thought would be the use of native prairie plants, i.e. sunflowers, prairie dock, big bluestem grass, coneflowers—all attractive plants that thrive in hot, dry environments.

Have all the options been considered for our common street? ▪

Greening Committee May Leaf Out Downtown

MARCH 9, 1983

Downtown Dayton will not become any greener this spring. Specific plans of the Green Downtown Dayton Committee have not progressed to the point of action that can be translated into more trees planted.

"Several things are on line," said Jack L. Ames, chairman of the committee and retired chairman of first National Bank, "but every phase of the large scale plan must be cleared by the City Planning Department, funds must be raised, landowner cooperation must be solicited and it look like this is not going to happen in time for spring planting."

It seems that planting a tree downtown is not a simple matter. The concrete and asphalt of the streets and sidewalks are on top of a maze of wires, cables, pipes and tunnels, necessitating a thorough check by the City Planning Department before clearance can be given to plant.

Harry Imboden, executive director of the Downtown Dayton Association, referring to the plan completed by the Harvard School of Design in 1981, pointed out the areas to be developed when clearance is received and funds permit.

The Fifth and Wilkinson Street area will be landscaped and some concrete work will be done to make the areas more attractive. Also, some benches may be added.

Fifth and Ludlow streets may be improved in similar fashion. Trees are to be planted at the Biltmore. Trees are also to be planted at the YMCA. Planting will be done from the Main Street Bridge south to the railroad overpass.

Ames pointed out the crucial need for funding on a large scale. This must be organized, and landowners canvassed to determine their attitude toward assisting with financing and maintaining plantings on their respective properties. In addition, donations must be sought from corporations and foundations to cover costs of planting.

John Gower, downtown planner for the City of Dayton, said the city has completed first phase conceptual plans for some of the current projects and has submitted these projects to the city administration for capital funding. This funding has been tentatively approved for submission to the city commission for final approval.

Capital funding from the city, when approved, will cover 20 percent of the cost of acquiring and planting 260 large trees over a period of four years at the various approved sites. Cost to the city (20%) would amount to $18,200 per year for the four-year period, or $72,800 total.

Gower said the Green Downtown Dayton Association must come up with 80% of the funds for planting and maintenance of the improved areas before the action stage is resumed.

The committee was formed in 1979 to develop a favorable plan for using street trees downtown to improve air quality, reduce energy consumption and noise levels, and to increase human comfort. ▪

Downtown Nature Stories Thrive Over the Years

What is natural about downtown Dayton?

That was the question I asked in my first column in the *Downtowner* on September 29, 1982.

> *"Let me adjust your attitude, pique your perspective, and titillate your thoughts by inviting you to get to know the wildlife, trees, birds, insects, critters of the river and even the geology of downtown Dayton.*
>
> *"...I'll provide you with seasonal overviews of natural happenings in the downtown area from every vantage point from the bottom of the river to the top of Kettering Tower and for a radius of about two miles in any direction from Third and Main Streets."*

The above was, in part, my first column for the Downtowner. I've had a ball covering the downtown wildlife "beat."

Imagine my surprise to find white-tailed deer swimming the Great Miami just below the Main Street bridge, great horned owls roosting on Arcade air vents, and an elderly ex-marine, Eddie Creighton, picking up a sparrow hawk and nursing it back to health in his Ludlow Street apartment. (At that time it was the Moraine Apartments, and it is now the Ludlow Manor.)

Everyone was amazed to find Rachel and Mercury, the original downtown peregrine falcons, inhabiting the old Lazarus building at Second and Ludlow Streets. Heading the list of "most amazed" was Mike Toephler, game manager with the Ohio Division of Wildlife. Mike was making plans to release falcons in Dayton in the spring of 1992 when this pair arrived, one from Columbus and one from Cincinnati. They became romantically involved, nested, and produced offspring.

A peak event was the discovery of rare yellow-crowned night herons at the mouth of Wolf Creek, on the Miami River at the Third Street Bridge, witnessed by several members of the Dayton Audubon Society.

To borrow a line from an auctioneer, "There are many other items too numerous to mention." It is true, there are enough exciting wildlife stories to write a book.

The idea for the Downtown Naturalist column came from the late Jean Kappel in the early '80s. Jim Van Dyne, editor of the Neighbors section in **The Dayton Daily News** reviewed some of my writing and passed it on to Jim Nichols. He supported the idea and it was good for 650 columns.

Editor's Note: The Downtown Naturalist column has been a unique reading experience for the *Downtowner* readers. Dane Mutter has worked hard to write it week after week. He may, indeed, write a book. For his past efforts we thank him, for his dreams, we hope they all come true. ■

About the Author

Dane Mutter has been a major player in the region's conservation and land stewardship progress. In 1963 he began working for the National Audubon Society as Director of the Aullwood Children's Farm, now Aullwood Audubon Farm and Center.

In 1967 he joined the Dayton-Montgomery County Park District, now Five Rivers MetroParks. He stayed with this organization as Associate Director until 1988, and then served as Executive Director of the newly formed Beavercreek Wetlands Association.

While with the Park District he started writing his weekly column, *Downtown Naturalist*, for the *Dayton Downtowner*, a supplement to the *Dayton Daily News*. He wrote his column for 13 years.

In 2007 he and Brian Hackett of The Dayton Historical Society published the book, *Gems of the Greater Dayton Region*, an overview of the natural and cultural history of our region.

In 2011 Dane was awarded the lifetime achievement award by the Partners for the Environment, a coalition of environmental organizations in the Miami Valley. And in 2018 the Beavercreek Wetlands Association named a newly created prairie the Dane Mutter Prairie.

Today Dane lives near the Stillwater River, which flows by his house. Though retired, he still spends as much time as possible outdoors. You may run into him out on the trail somewhere. ∎

www.ingramcontent.com/pod-product-compliance
Lightning Source LLC
Chambersburg PA
CBHW052053270326
41931CB00012B/2738